STAR WARS

EPISODE I

THE PHANTOM MENACE

STAR WARS

EPISODE I

THE PHANTOM MENACE™

Adapted by

HENRY GILROY

from an original story by

GEORGE LUCAS

Pencils by

RODOLFO DAMAGGIO

with inks by

AL WILLIAMSON

DARK HORSE COMICS®

Episode I

THE PHANTOM MENACE

Turmoil has engulfed the Galactic Republic. The taxation of trade routes to outlying star systems is in dispute.

Hoping to resolve the matter with a blockade of deadly battleships, the greedy Trade Federation has stopped all shipping to the small planet of Naboo.

While the Congress of the Republic endlessly debates this alarming chain of events, the Supreme Chancellor has secretly dispatched two Jedi Knights, the guardians of peace and justice in the galaxy, to settle the conflict. . . .

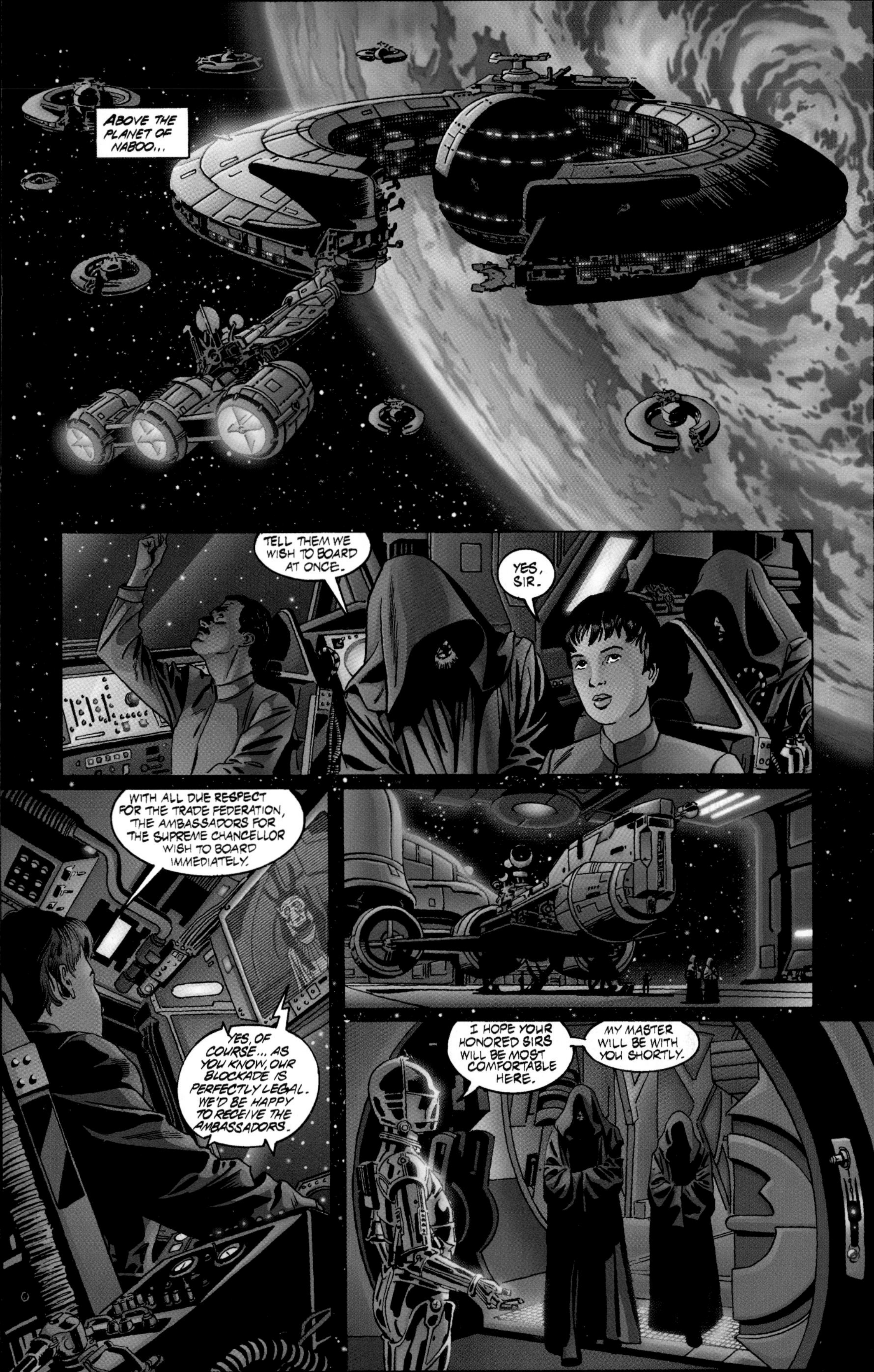
ABOVE THE PLANET OF NABOO...
TELL THEM WE WISH TO BOARD AT ONCE.
YES, SIR.
WITH ALL DUE RESPECT FOR THE TRADE FEDERATION, THE AMBASSADORS FOR THE SUPREME CHANCELLOR WISH TO BOARD IMMEDIATELY.
YES, OF COURSE... AS YOU KNOW, OUR BLOCKADE IS PERFECTLY LEGAL. WE'D BE HAPPY TO RECEIVE THE AMBASSADORS.
I HOPE YOUR HONORED SIRS WILL BE MOST COMFORTABLE HERE.
MY MASTER WILL BE WITH YOU SHORTLY.

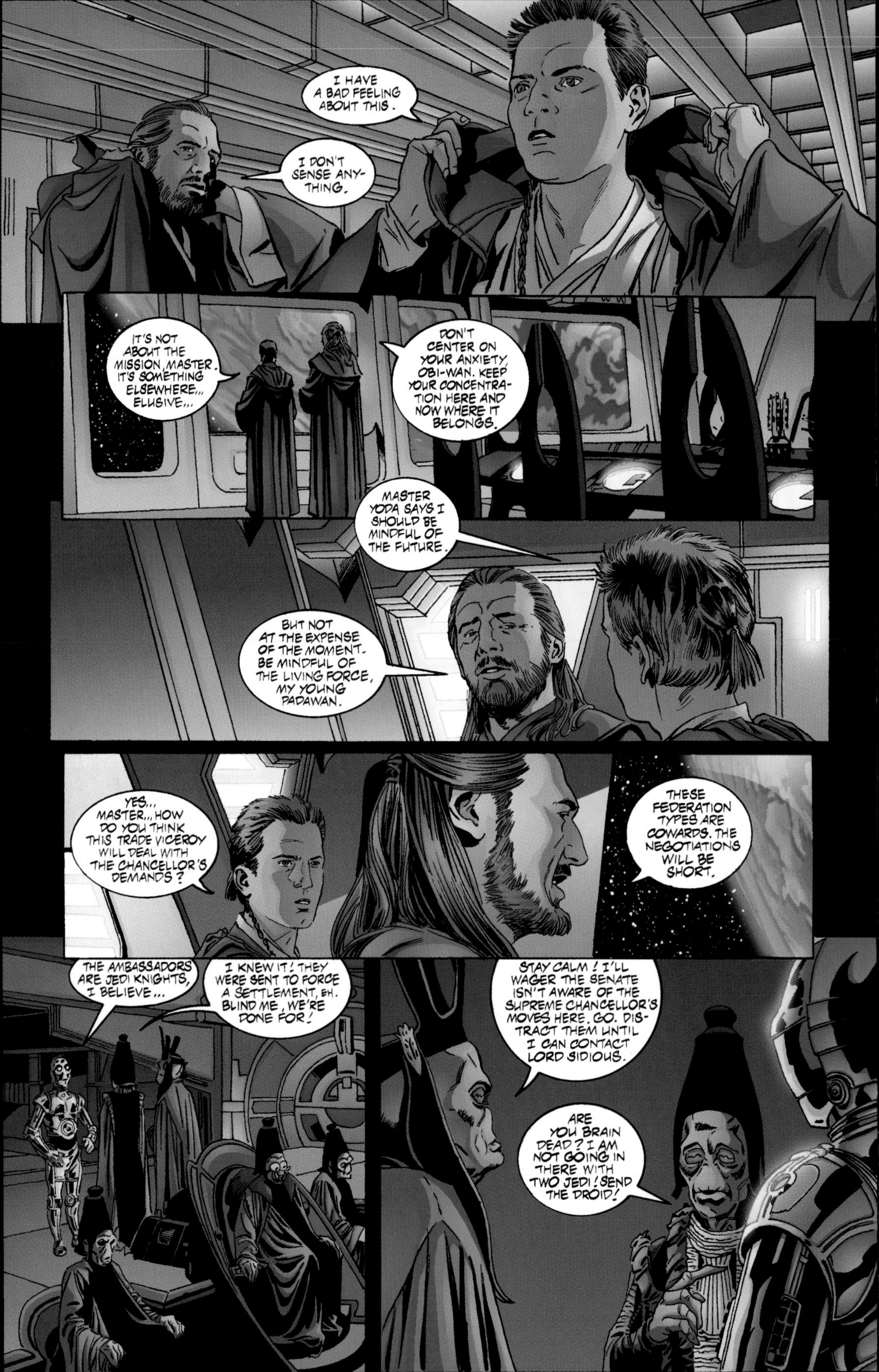
I HAVE A BAD FEELING ABOUT THIS.
I DON'T SENSE ANYTHING.
IT'S NOT ABOUT THE MISSION, MASTER. IT'S SOMETHING ELSEWHERE... ELUSIVE...
DON'T CENTER ON YOUR ANXIETY, OBI-WAN. KEEP YOUR CONCENTRATION HERE AND NOW WHERE IT BELONGS.
MASTER YODA SAYS I SHOULD BE MINDFUL OF THE FUTURE.
BUT NOT AT THE EXPENSE OF THE MOMENT. BE MINDFUL OF THE LIVING FORCE, MY YOUNG PADAWAN.
YES... MASTER... HOW DO YOU THINK THIS TRADE VICEROY WILL DEAL WITH THE CHANCELLOR'S DEMANDS?
THESE FEDERATION TYPES ARE COWARDS. THE NEGOTIATIONS WILL BE SHORT.
THE AMBASSADORS ARE JEDI KNIGHTS, I BELIEVE...
I KNEW IT! THEY WERE SENT TO FORCE A SETTLEMENT, EH. BLIND ME, WE'RE DONE FOR!
STAY CALM! I'LL WAGER THE SENATE ISN'T AWARE OF THE SUPREME CHANCELLOR'S MOVES HERE. GO. DISTRACT THEM UNTIL I CAN CONTACT LORD SIDIOUS.
ARE YOU BRAIN DEAD? I AM NOT GOING IN THERE WITH TWO JEDI! SEND THE DROID!

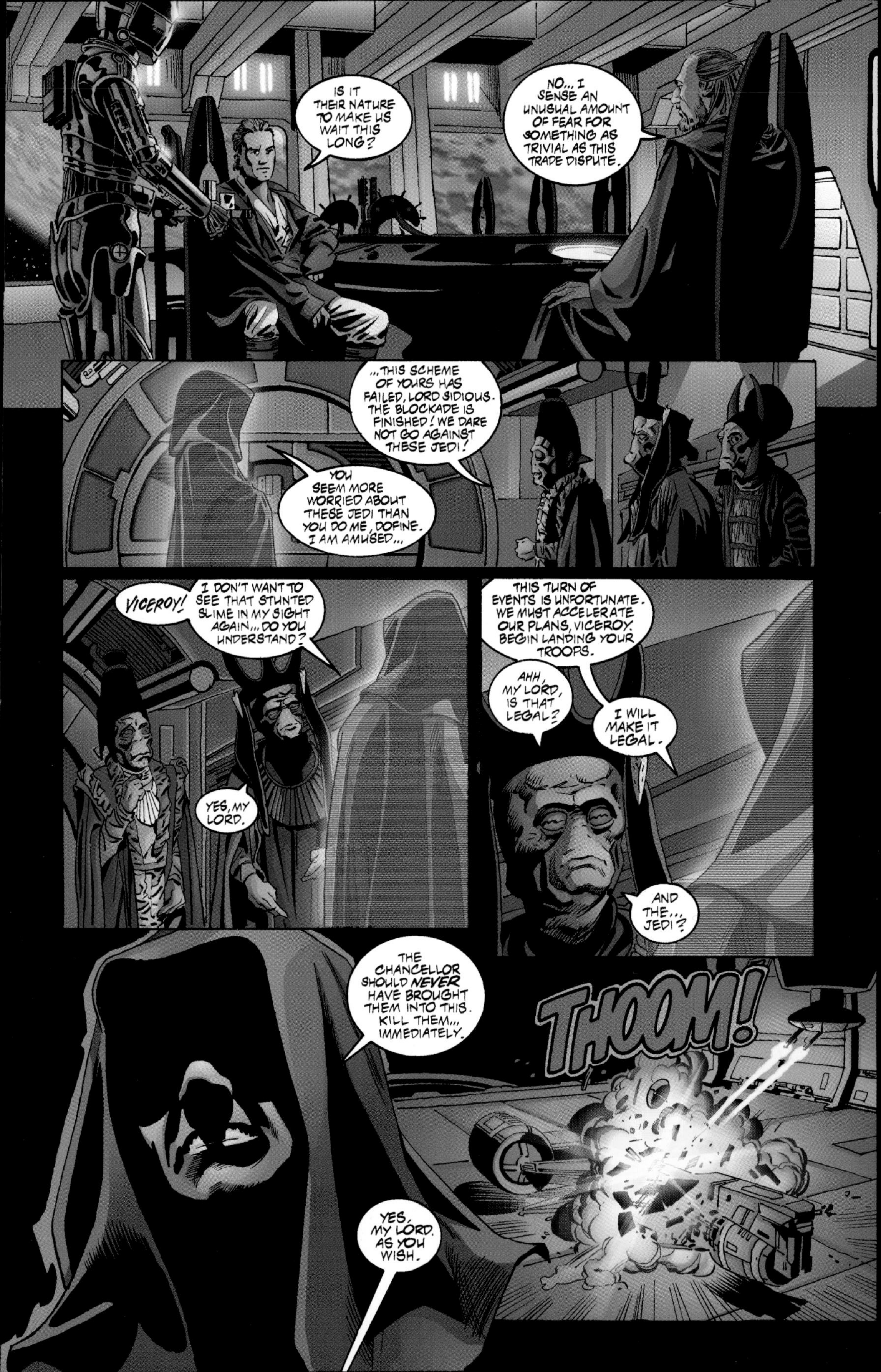
IS IT THEIR NATURE TO MAKE US WAIT THIS LONG?
NO... I SENSE AN UNUSUAL AMOUNT OF FEAR FOR SOMETHING AS TRIVIAL AS THIS TRADE DISPUTE.
...THIS SCHEME OF YOURS HAS FAILED, LORD SIDIOUS. THE BLOCKADE IS FINISHED! WE DARE NOT GO AGAINST THESE JEDI!
YOU SEEM MORE WORRIED ABOUT THESE JEDI THAN YOU DO ME, DOFINE. I AM AMUSED...
VICEROY!
I DON'T WANT TO SEE THAT STUNTED SLIME IN MY SIGHT AGAIN... DO YOU UNDERSTAND?
YES, MY LORD.
THIS TURN OF EVENTS IS UNFORTUNATE. WE MUST ACCELERATE OUR PLANS, VICEROY. BEGIN LANDING YOUR TROOPS.
AHH, MY LORD, IS THAT LEGAL?
I WILL MAKE IT LEGAL.
AND THE... JEDI?
THE CHANCELLOR SHOULD NEVER HAVE BROUGHT THEM INTO THIS. KILL THEM... IMMEDIATELY.
YES, MY LORD. AS YOU WISH.
THOOM!

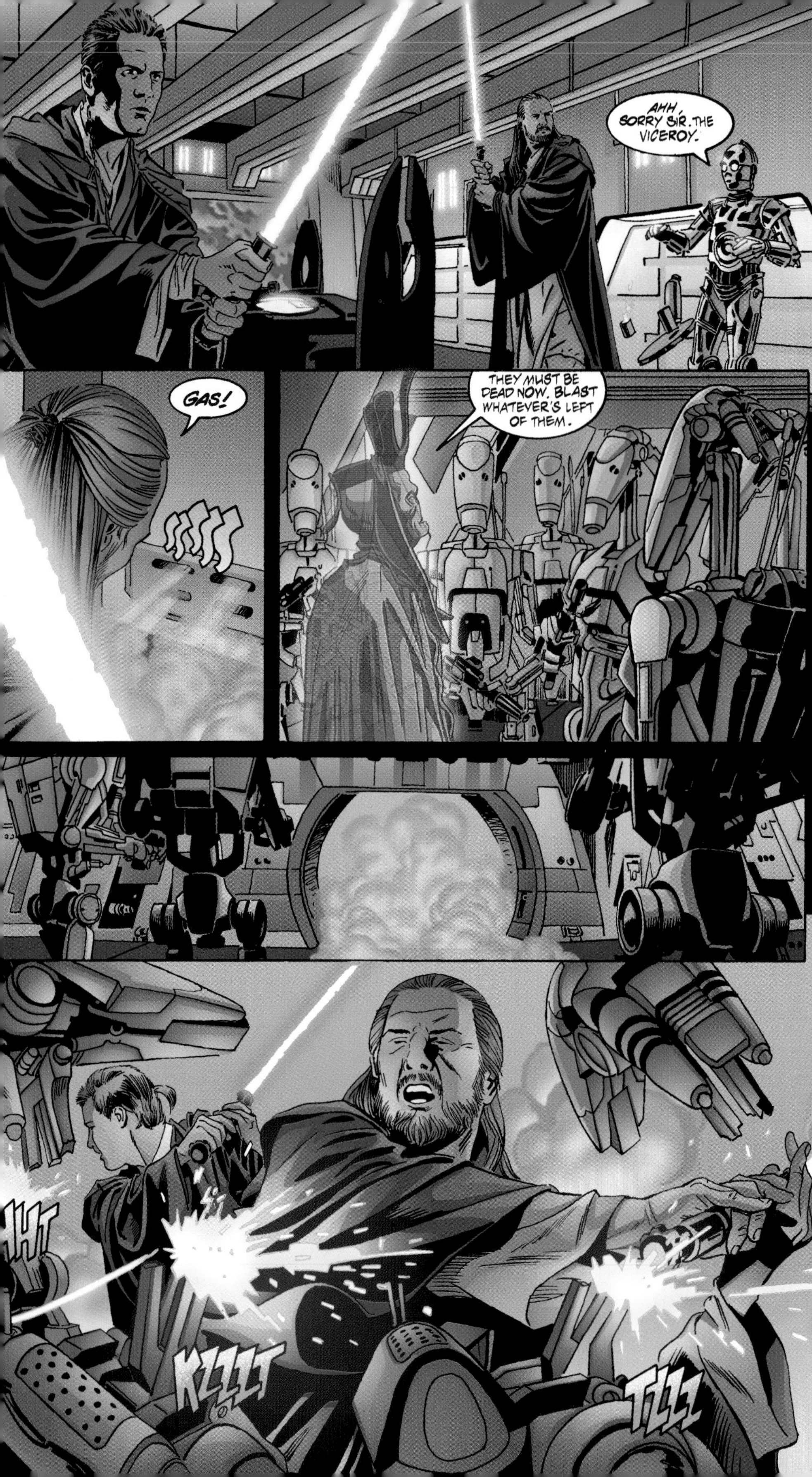
AHH, SORRY SIR. THE VICEROY.
GAS!
SSSS
THEY MUST BE DEAD NOW. BLAST WHATEVER'S LEFT OF THEM.
KZZZT
TZZZ

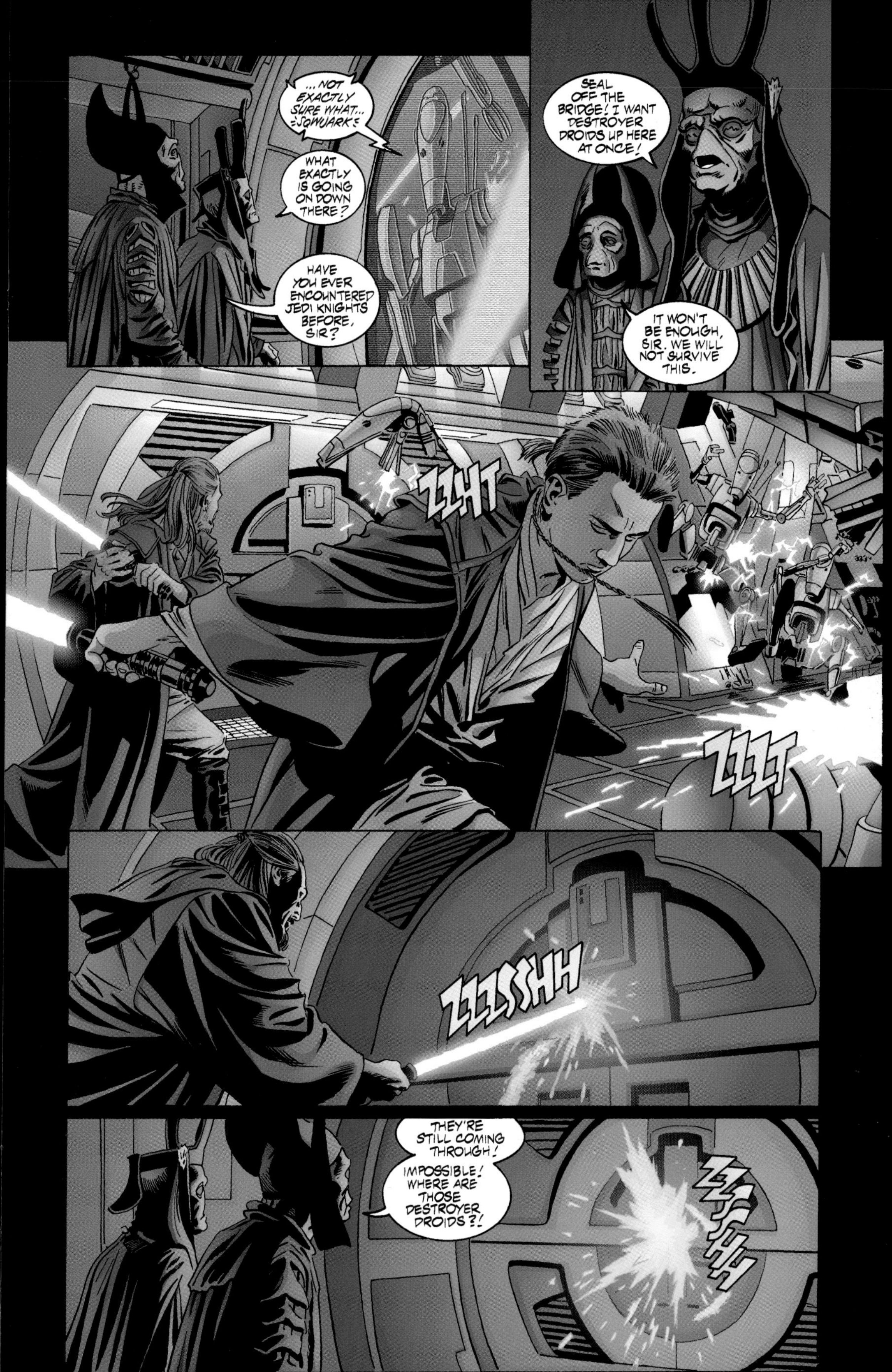
...NOT EXACTLY SURE WHAT... =SQWUARK=
WHAT EXACTLY IS GOING ON DOWN THERE?
HAVE YOU EVER ENCOUNTERED JEDI KNIGHTS BEFORE, SIR?
SEAL OFF THE BRIDGE! I WANT DESTROYER DROIDS UP HERE AT ONCE!
IT WON'T BE ENOUGH, SIR. WE WILL NOT SURVIVE THIS.
ZZZHT
ZZZT
ZZZSSHH
THEY'RE STILL COMING THROUGH!
IMPOSSIBLE! WHERE ARE THOSE DESTROYER DROIDS?!
ZZSSHH

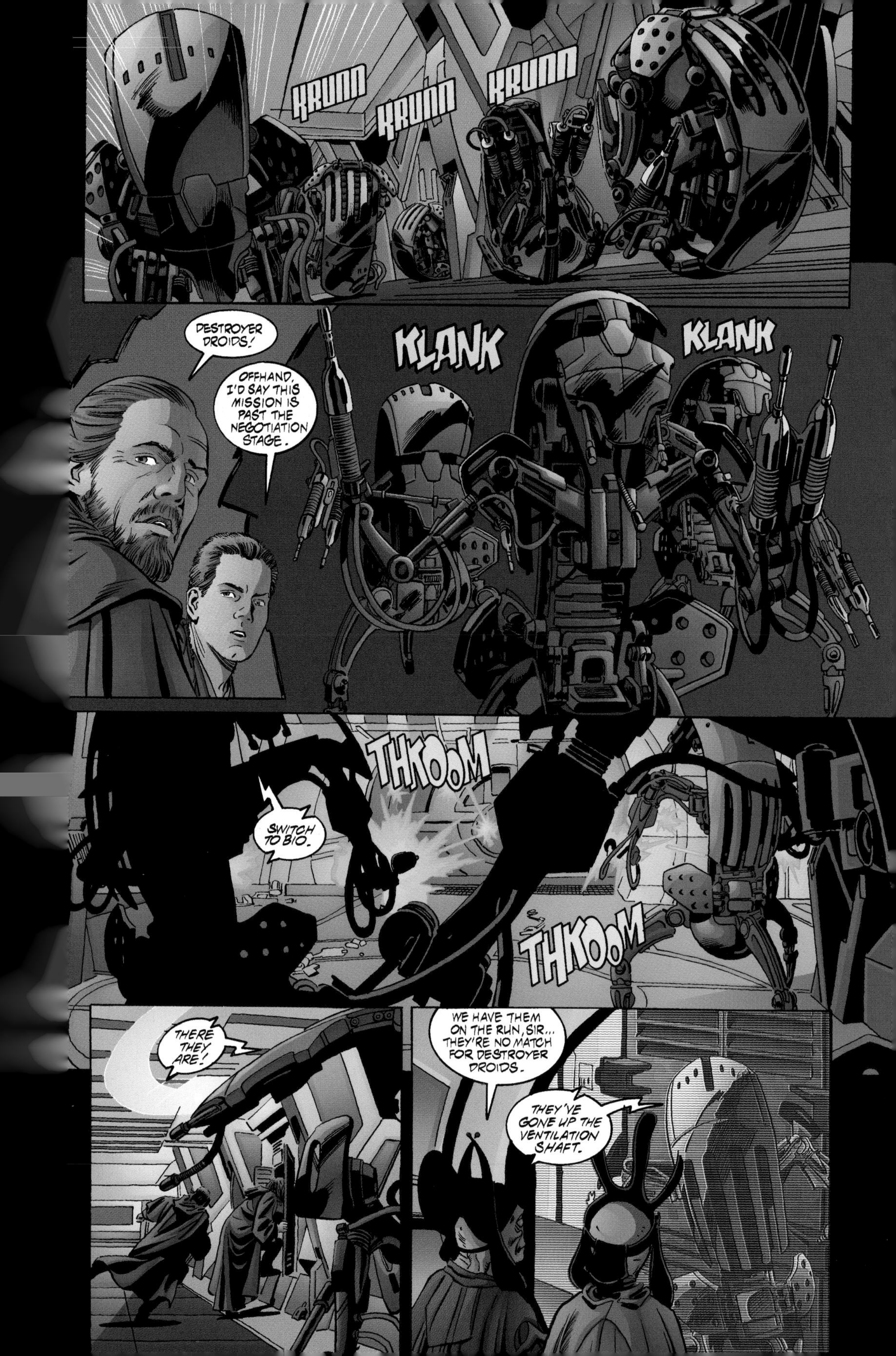
KRUNN
KRUNN
KRUNN
DESTROYER DROIDS!
OFFHAND, I'D SAY THIS MISSION IS PAST THE NEGOTIATION STAGE.
KLANK
KLANK
THKOOM
SWITCH TO BIO.
THKOOM
THERE THEY ARE!
WE HAVE THEM ON THE RUN, SIR... THEY'RE NO MATCH FOR DESTROYER DROIDS.
THEY'VE GONE UP THE VENTILATION SHAFT.

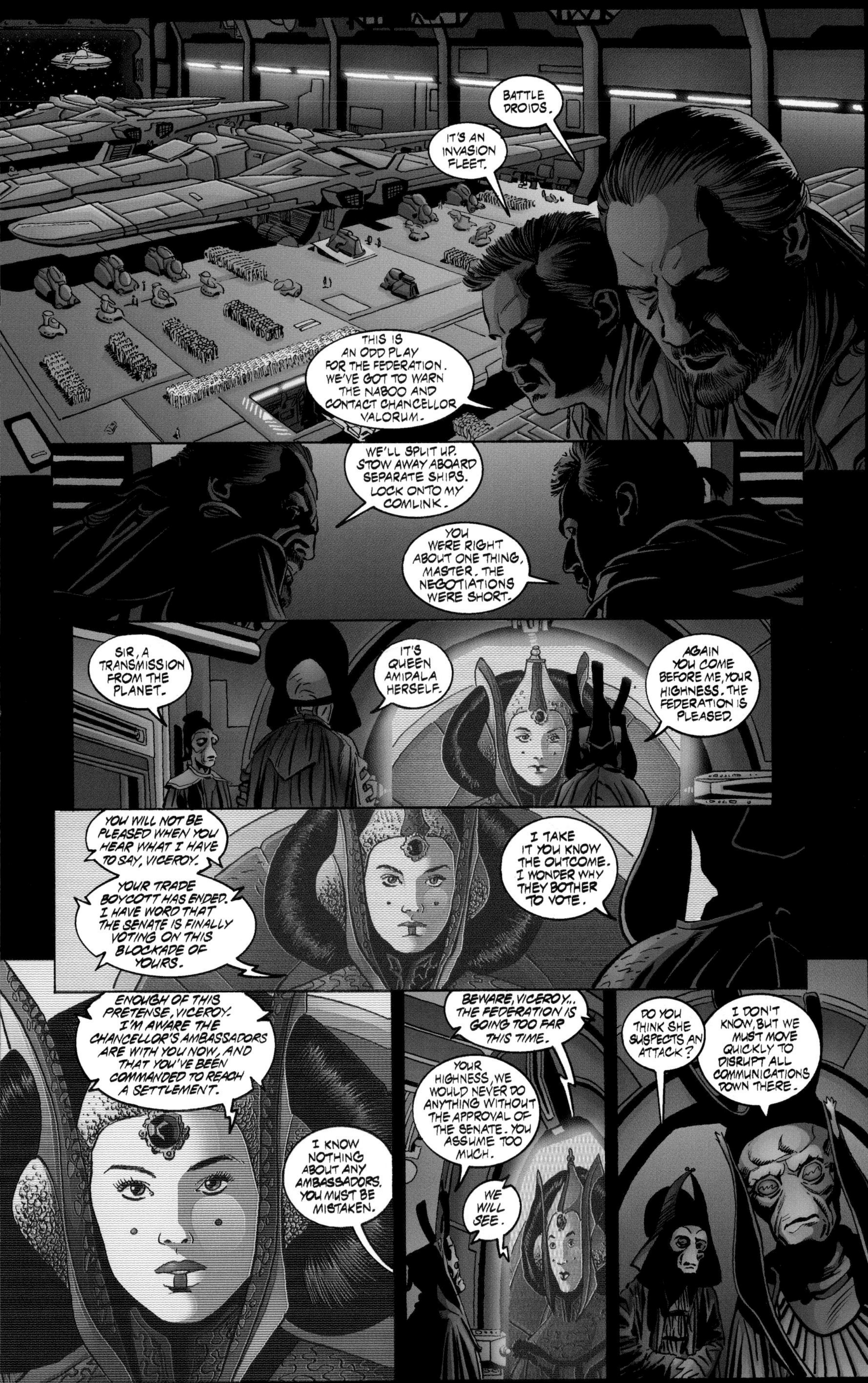
BATTLE DROIDS.
IT'S AN INVASION FLEET.
THIS IS AN ODD PLAY FOR THE FEDERATION. WE'VE GOT TO WARN THE NABOO AND CONTACT CHANCELLOR VALORUM.
WE'LL SPLIT UP. STOW AWAY ABOARD SEPARATE SHIPS. LOCK ONTO MY COMLINK.
YOU WERE RIGHT ABOUT ONE THING, MASTER. THE NEGOTIATIONS WERE SHORT.
SIR, A TRANSMISSION FROM THE PLANET.
IT'S QUEEN AMIDALA HERSELF.
AGAIN YOU COME BEFORE ME, YOUR HIGHNESS. THE FEDERATION IS PLEASED.
YOU WILL NOT BE PLEASED WHEN YOU HEAR WHAT I HAVE TO SAY, VICEROY.
YOUR TRADE BOYCOTT HAS ENDED. I HAVE WORD THAT THE SENATE IS FINALLY VOTING ON THIS BLOCKADE OF YOURS.
I TAKE IT YOU KNOW THE OUTCOME. I WONDER WHY THEY BOTHER TO VOTE.
ENOUGH OF THIS PRETENSE, VICEROY. I'M AWARE THE CHANCELLOR'S AMBASSADORS ARE WITH YOU NOW, AND THAT YOU'VE BEEN COMMANDED TO REACH A SETTLEMENT.
I KNOW NOTHING ABOUT ANY AMBASSADORS. YOU MUST BE MISTAKEN.
BEWARE, VICEROY... THE FEDERATION IS GOING TOO FAR THIS TIME.
YOUR HIGHNESS, WE WOULD NEVER DO ANYTHING WITHOUT THE APPROVAL OF THE SENATE. YOU ASSUME TOO MUCH.
WE WILL SEE.
DO YOU THINK SHE SUSPECTS AN ATTACK?
I DON'T KNOW, BUT WE MUST MOVE QUICKLY TO DISRUPT ALL COMMUNICATIONS DOWN THERE.

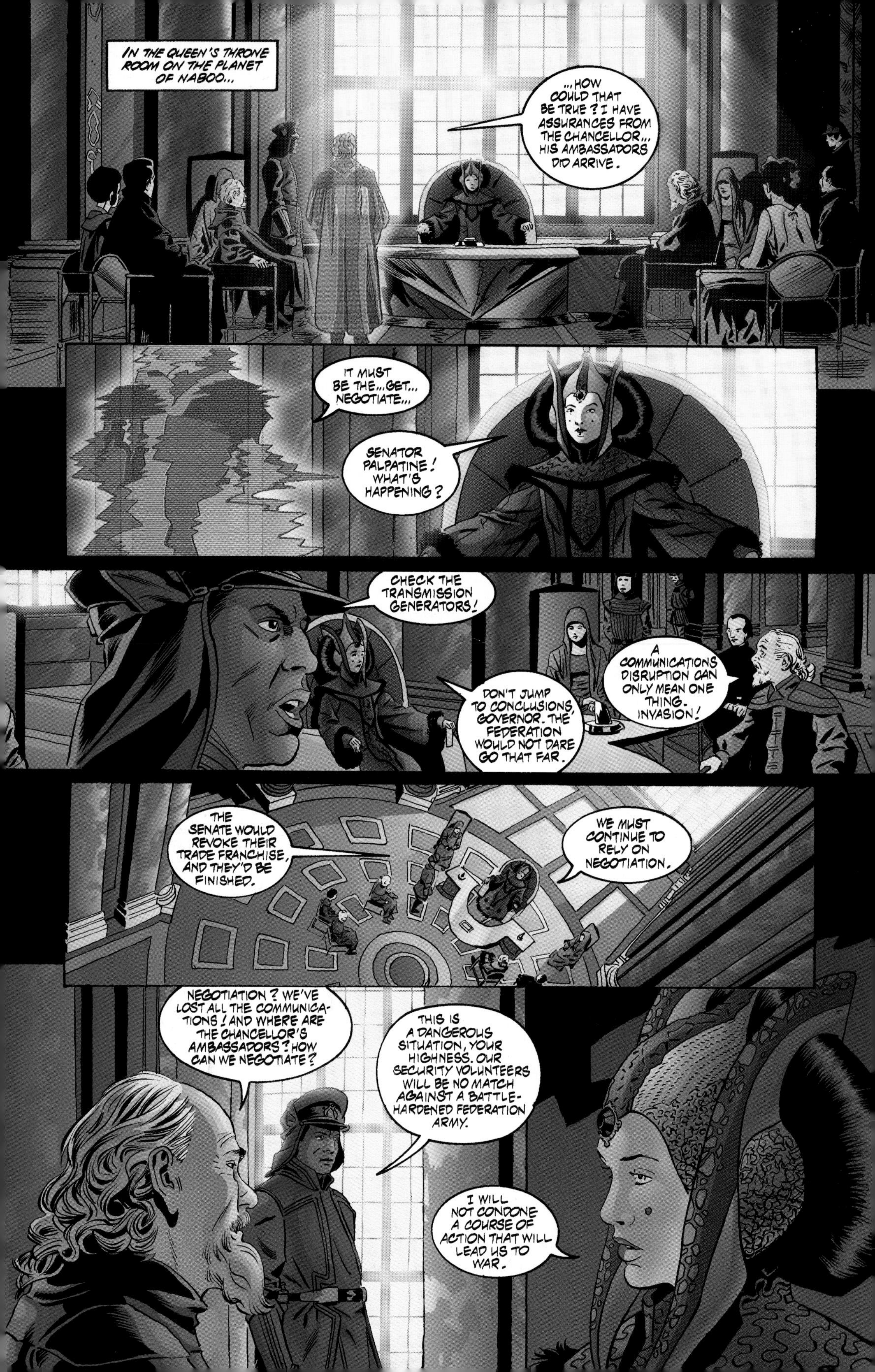
IN THE QUEEN'S THRONE ROOM ON THE PLANET OF NABOO...
...HOW COULD THAT BE TRUE? I HAVE ASSURANCES FROM THE CHANCELLOR... HIS AMBASSADORS DID ARRIVE.
IT MUST BE THE...GET... NEGOTIATE...
SENATOR PALPATINE! WHAT'S HAPPENING?
CHECK THE TRANSMISSION GENERATORS!
A COMMUNICATIONS DISRUPTION CAN ONLY MEAN ONE THING. INVASION!
DON'T JUMP TO CONCLUSIONS, GOVERNOR. THE FEDERATION WOULD NOT DARE GO THAT FAR.
THE SENATE WOULD REVOKE THEIR TRADE FRANCHISE, AND THEY'D BE FINISHED.
WE MUST CONTINUE TO RELY ON NEGOTIATION.
NEGOTIATION? WE'VE LOST ALL THE COMMUNICATIONS! AND WHERE ARE THE CHANCELLOR'S AMBASSADORS? HOW CAN WE NEGOTIATE?
THIS IS A DANGEROUS SITUATION, YOUR HIGHNESS. OUR SECURITY VOLUNTEERS WILL BE NO MATCH AGAINST A BATTLE-HARDENED FEDERATION ARMY.
I WILL NOT CONDONE A COURSE OF ACTION THAT WILL LEAD US TO WAR.

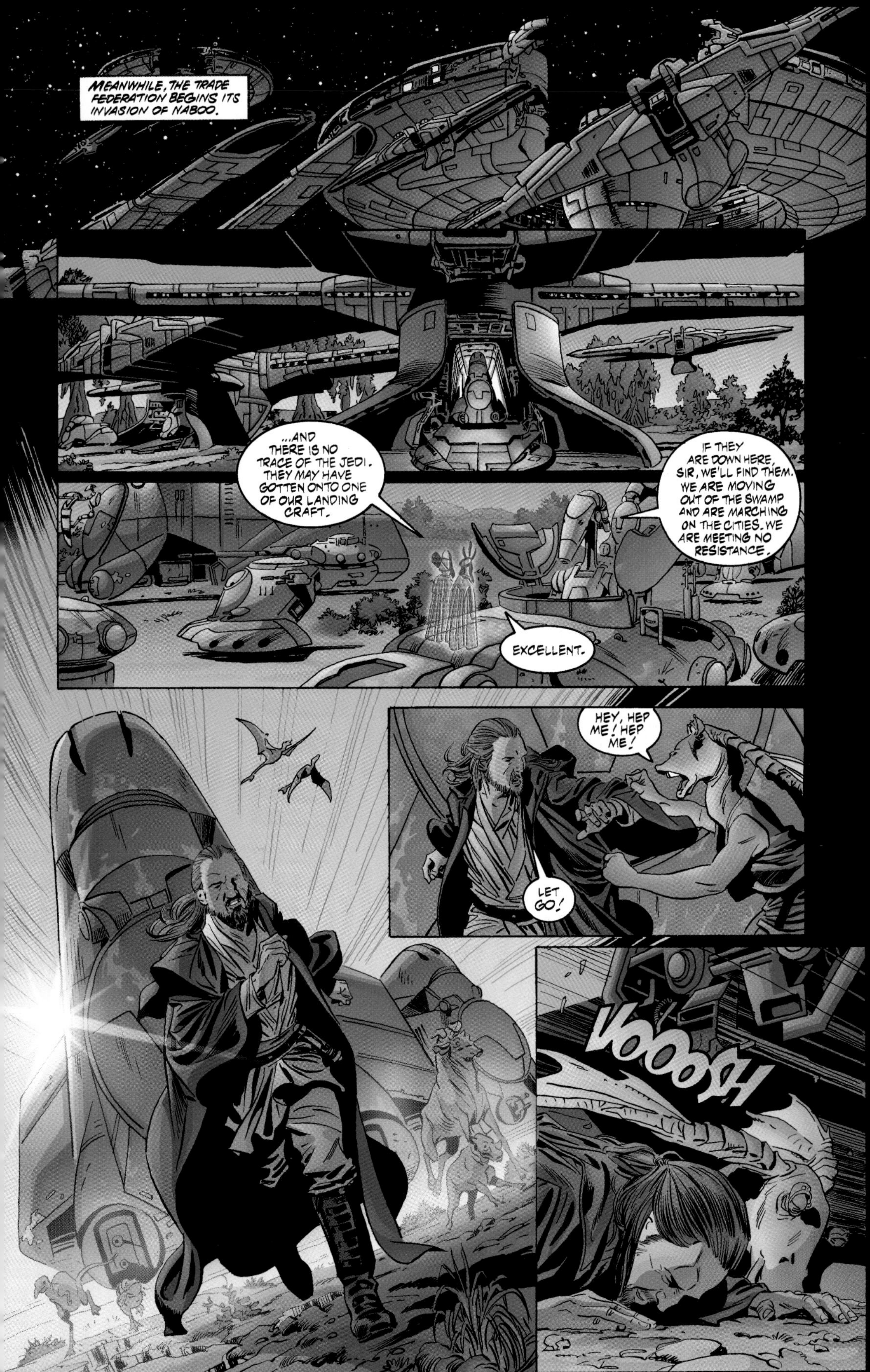
MEANWHILE, THE TRADE FEDERATION BEGINS ITS INVASION OF NABOO.
...AND THERE IS NO TRACE OF THE JEDI. THEY MAY HAVE GOTTEN ONTO ONE OF OUR LANDING CRAFT.
IF THEY ARE DOWN HERE, SIR, WE'LL FIND THEM. WE ARE MOVING OUT OF THE SWAMP AND ARE MARCHING ON THE CITIES. WE ARE MEETING NO RESISTANCE.
EXCELLENT.
HEY, HEP ME! HEP ME!
LET GO!
VOOOSH

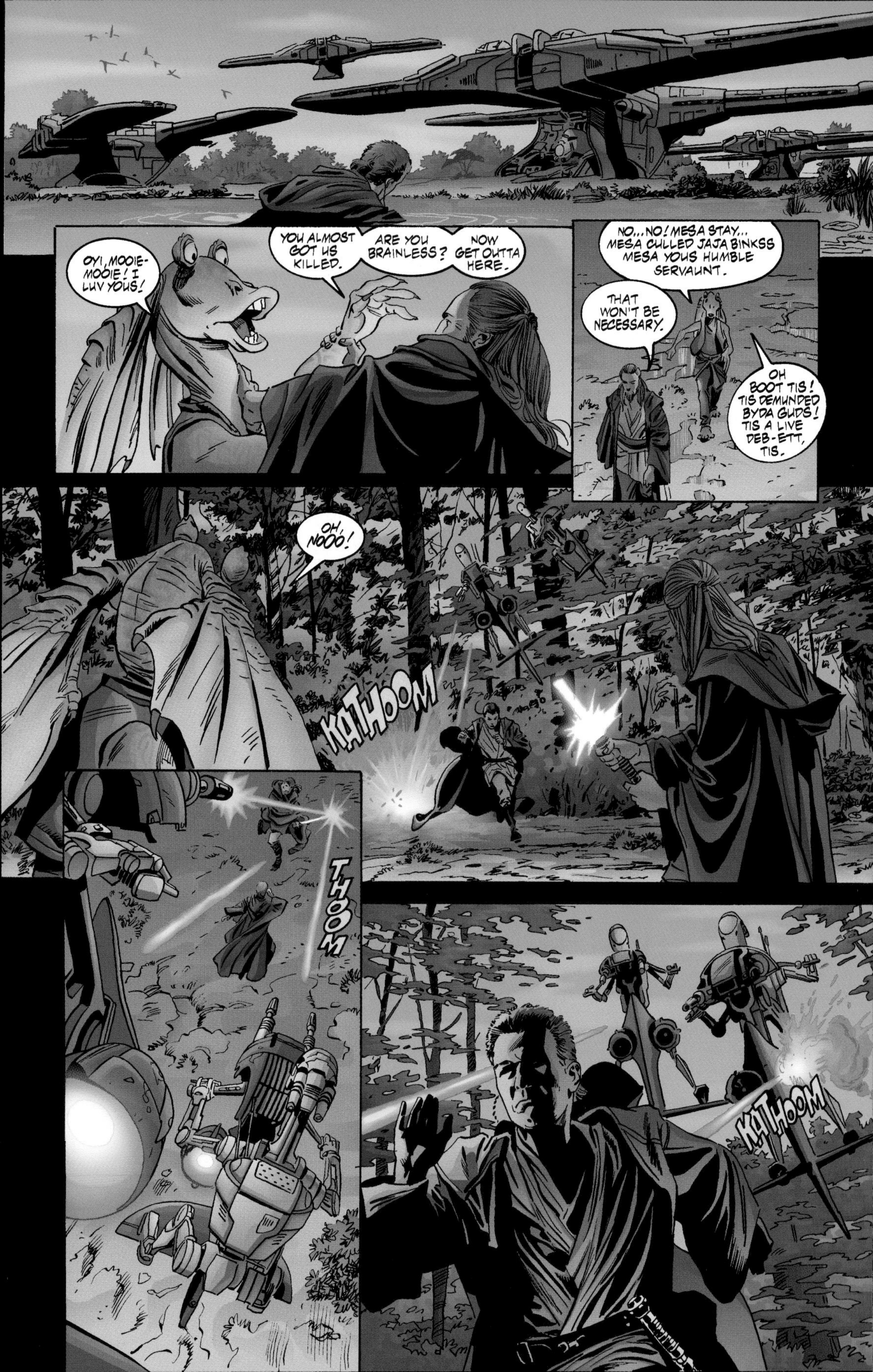
OY! MOOIE-MOOIE! I LUV YOUS!
YOU ALMOST GOT US KILLED.
ARE YOU BRAINLESS?
NOW GET OUTTA HERE.
NO... NO! MESA STAY... MESA CULLED JAJA BINKSS MESA YOUS HUMBLE SERVAUNT.
THAT WON'T BE NECESSARY.
OH BOOT TIS! TIS DEMUNDED BYDA GUDS! TIS A LIVE DEB-ETT, TIS.
OH, NOOO!
KATHOOM
THOOM
KATHOOM

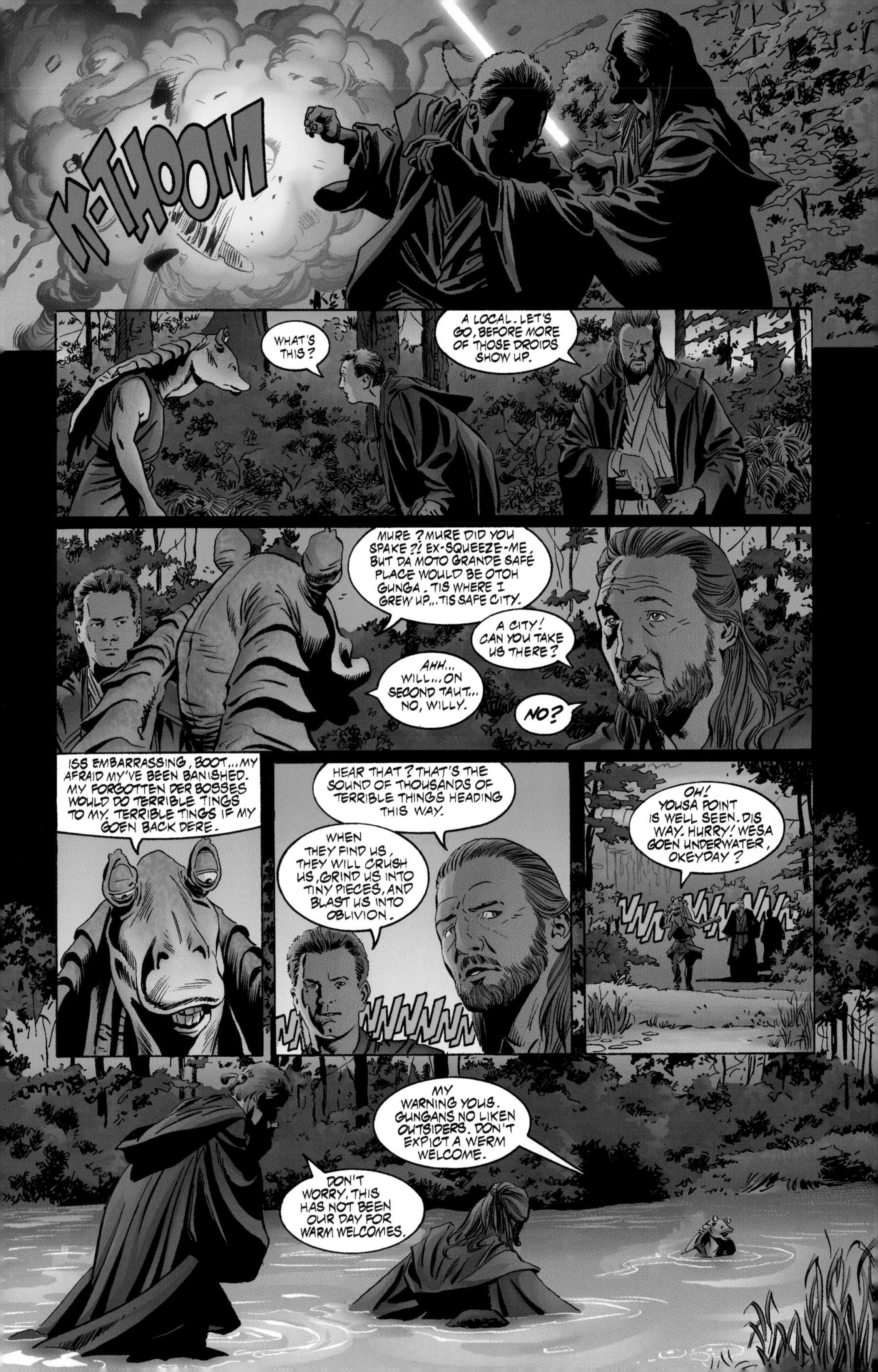
K-THOOM
WHAT'S THIS?
A LOCAL. LET'S GO, BEFORE MORE OF THOSE DROIDS SHOW UP.
MURE? MURE DID YOU SPAKE?! EX-SQUEEZE-ME, BUT DA MOTO GRANDE SAFÉ PLACE WOULD BE OTOH GUNGA. TIS WHERE I GREW UP... TIS SAFE CITY.
A CITY! CAN YOU TAKE US THERE?
AHH... WILL... ON SECOND TAUT... NO, WILLY.
NO?
ISS EMBARRASSING, BOOT... MY AFRAID MY'VE BEEN BANISHED. MY FORGOTTEN DER BOSSES WOULD DO TERRIBLE TINGS TO MY. TERRIBLE TINGS IF MY GOEN BACK DERE.
HEAR THAT? THAT'S THE SOUND OF THOUSANDS OF TERRIBLE THINGS HEADING THIS WAY.
WHEN THEY FIND US, THEY WILL CRUSH US, GRIND US INTO TINY PIECES, AND BLAST US INTO OBLIVION.
NNNNNNN
OH! YOUSA POINT IS WELL SEEN. DIS WAY. HURRY! WESA GOEN UNDERWATER, OKEYDAY?
MY WARNING YOUS. GUNGANS NO LIKEN OUTSIDERS. DON'T EXPICT A WERM WELCOME.
DON'T WORRY, THIS HAS NOT BEEN OUR DAY FOR WARM WELCOMES.

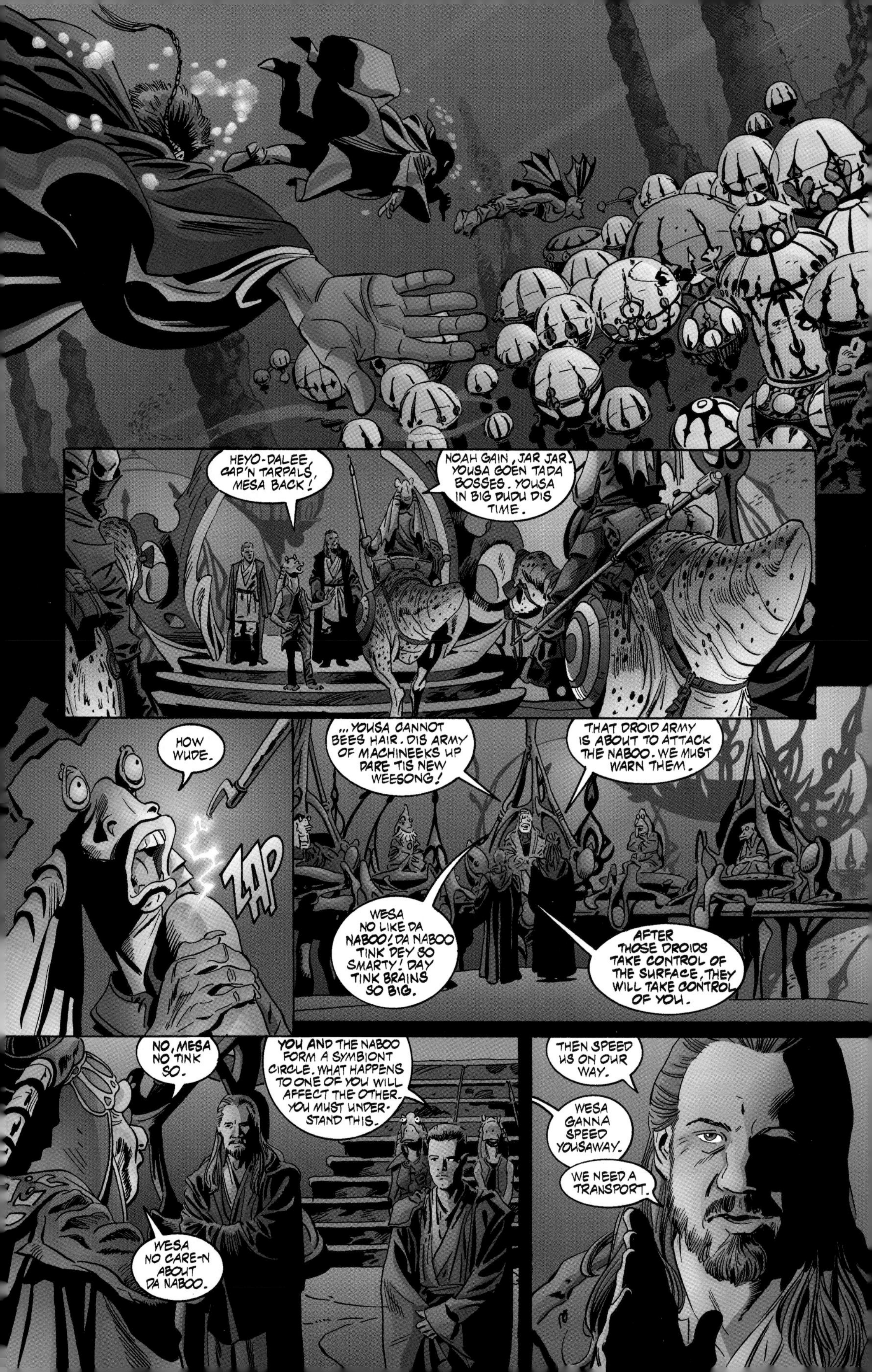
HEYO-DALEE, CAP'N TARPALS, MESA BACK!
NOAH GAIN, JAR JAR. YOUSA GOEN TADA BOSSES. YOUSA IN BIG DUDU DIS TIME.
HOW WUDE.
ZAP
...YOUSA CANNOT BEES HAIR. DIS ARMY OF MACHINEEKS UP DARE TIS NEW WEESONG!
THAT DROID ARMY IS ABOUT TO ATTACK THE NABOO. WE MUST WARN THEM.
WESA NO LIKE DA NABOO! DA NABOO TINK DEY SO SMARTY! DAY TINK BRAINS SO BIG.
AFTER THOSE DROIDS TAKE CONTROL OF THE SURFACE, THEY WILL TAKE CONTROL OF YOU.
NO, MESA NO TINK SO.
YOU AND THE NABOO FORM A SYMBIONT CIRCLE. WHAT HAPPENS TO ONE OF YOU WILL AFFECT THE OTHER. YOU MUST UNDERSTAND THIS.
WESA NO CARE-N ABOUT DA NABOO.
THEN SPEED US ON OUR WAY.
WESA GANNA SPEED YOUSAWAY.
WE NEED A TRANSPORT.

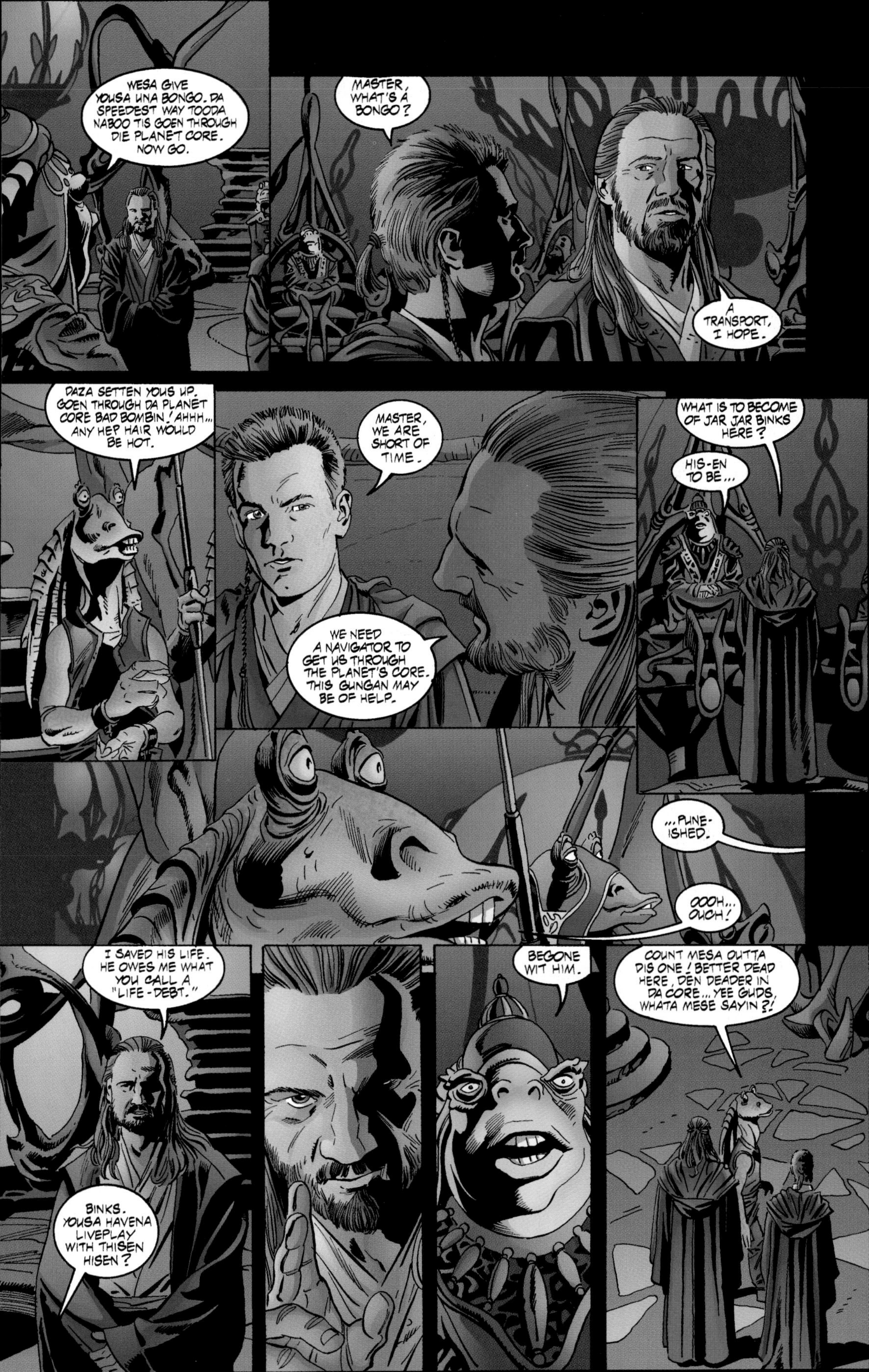
WESA GIVE YOUSA UNA BONGO. DA SPEEDEST WAY TOODA NABOO TIS GOEN THROUGH DIE PLANET CORE. NOW GO.
MASTER, WHAT'S A BONGO?
A TRANSPORT, I HOPE.
DAZA SETTEN YOUS UP. GOEN THROUGH DA PLANET CORE BAD BOMBIN! AHHH... ANY HEP HAIR WOULD BE HOT.
MASTER, WE ARE SHORT OF TIME.
WE NEED A NAVIGATOR TO GET US THROUGH THE PLANET'S CORE. THIS GUNGAN MAY BE OF HELP.
WHAT IS TO BECOME OF JAR JAR BINKS HERE?
HIS-EN TO BE...
...PUNE-ISHED.
OOOH... OUCH!
I SAVED HIS LIFE. HE OWES ME WHAT YOU CALL A "LIFE-DEBT."
BINKS. YOUSA HAVENA LIVEPLAY WITH THISEN HISEN?
BEGONE WIT HIM.
COUNT MESA OUTTA DIS ONE! BETTER DEAD HERE, DEN DEADER IN DA CORE... YEE GUDS, WHATA MESE SAYIN?!

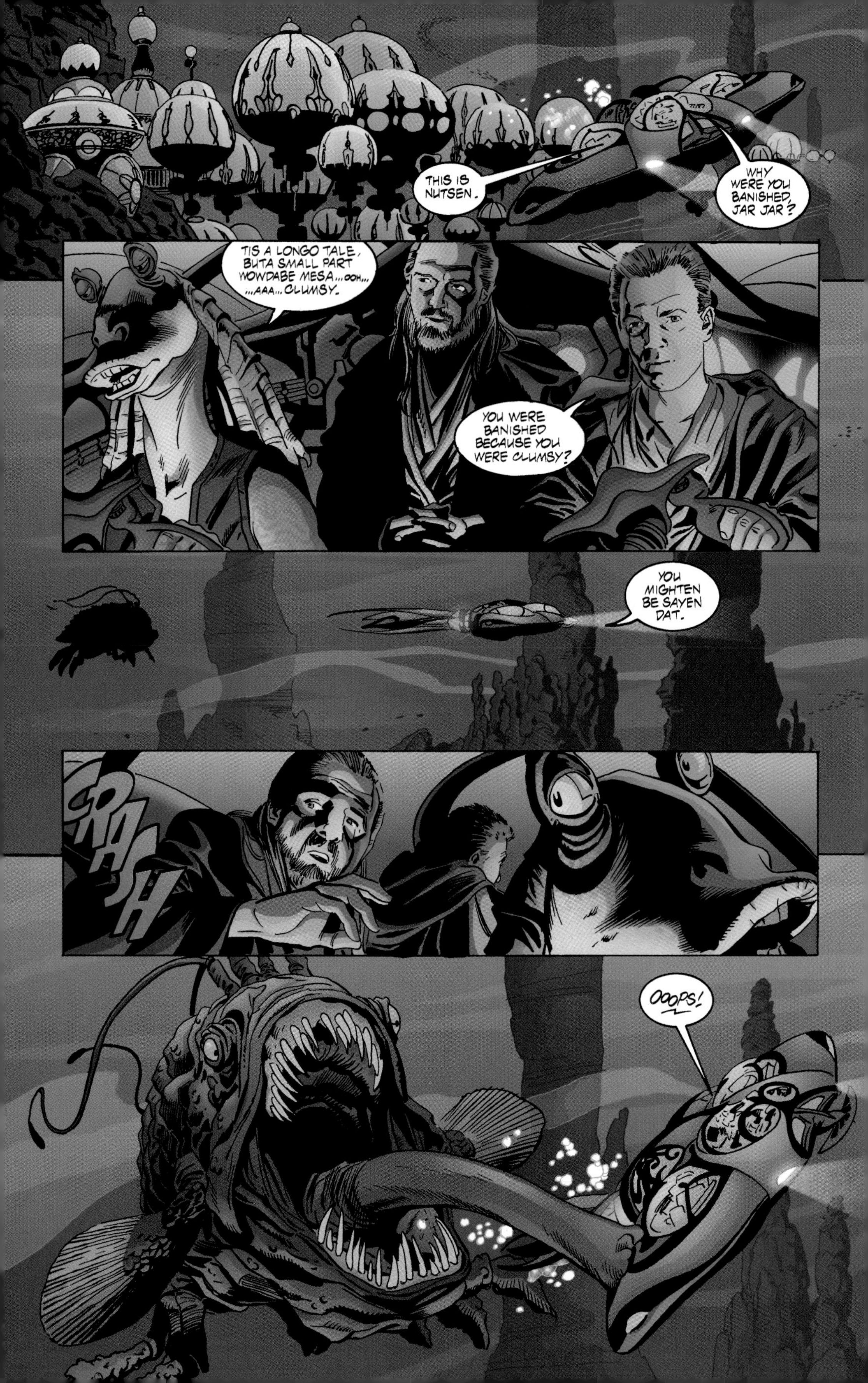
THIS IS NUTSEN.
WHY WERE YOU BANISHED, JAR JAR?
TIS A LONGO TALE, BUTA SMALL PART WOWDABE MESA...OOH... ...AAA...CLUMSY.
YOU WERE BANISHED BECAUSE YOU WERE CLUMSY?
YOU MIGHTEN BE SAYEN DAT.
CRASH
OOOPS!

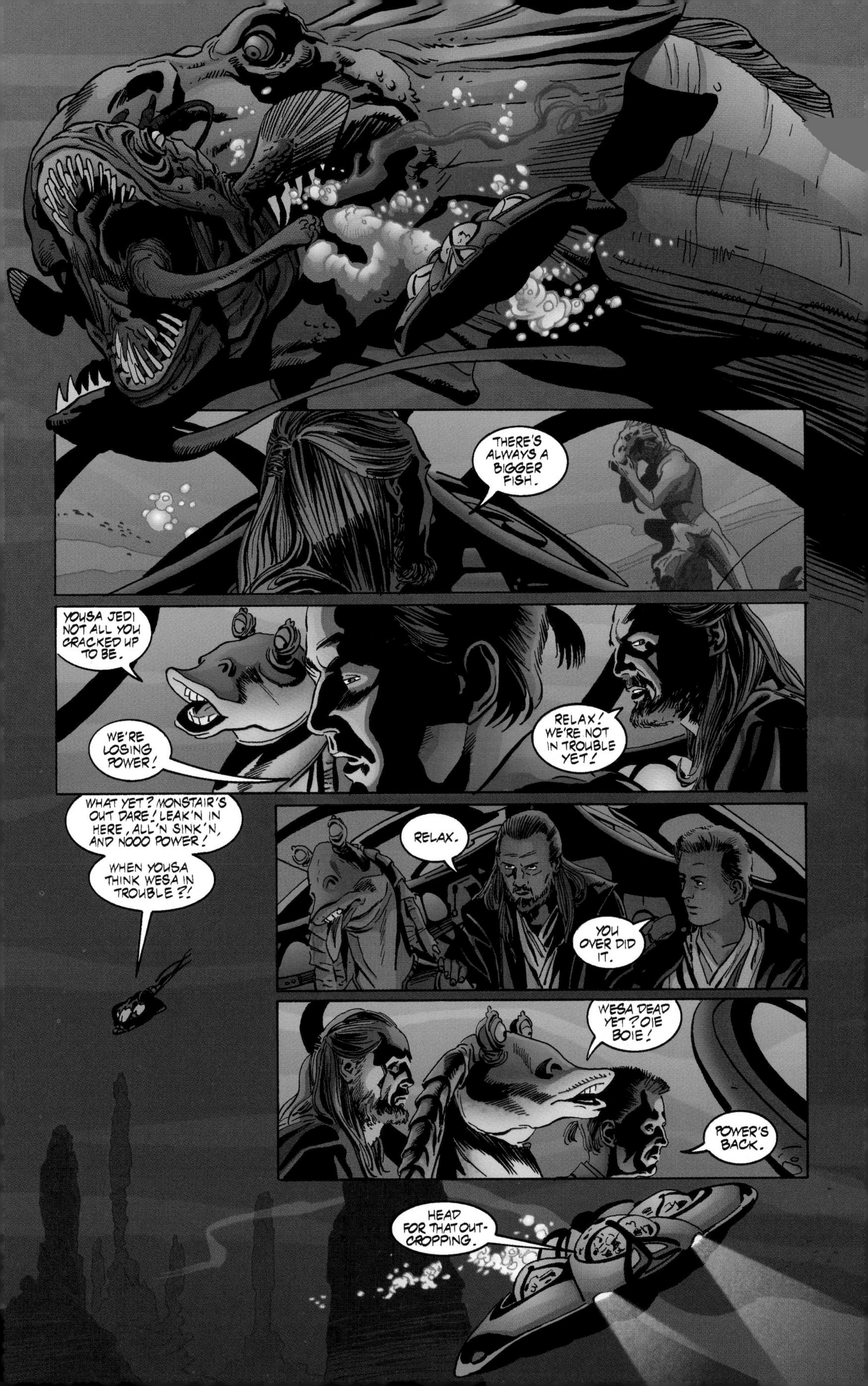
THERE'S ALWAYS A BIGGER FISH.
YOUSA JEDI NOT ALL YOU CRACKED UP TO BE.
WE'RE LOSING POWER!
RELAX! WE'RE NOT IN TROUBLE YET!
WHAT YET? MONSTAIR'S OUT DARE! LEAK'N IN HERE, ALL'N SINK'N, AND NOOO POWER!
WHEN YOUSA THINK WESA IN TROUBLE?!
RELAX.
YOU OVER DID IT.
WESA DEAD YET? OIE BOIE!
POWER'S BACK.
HEAD FOR THAT OUT-CROPPING.

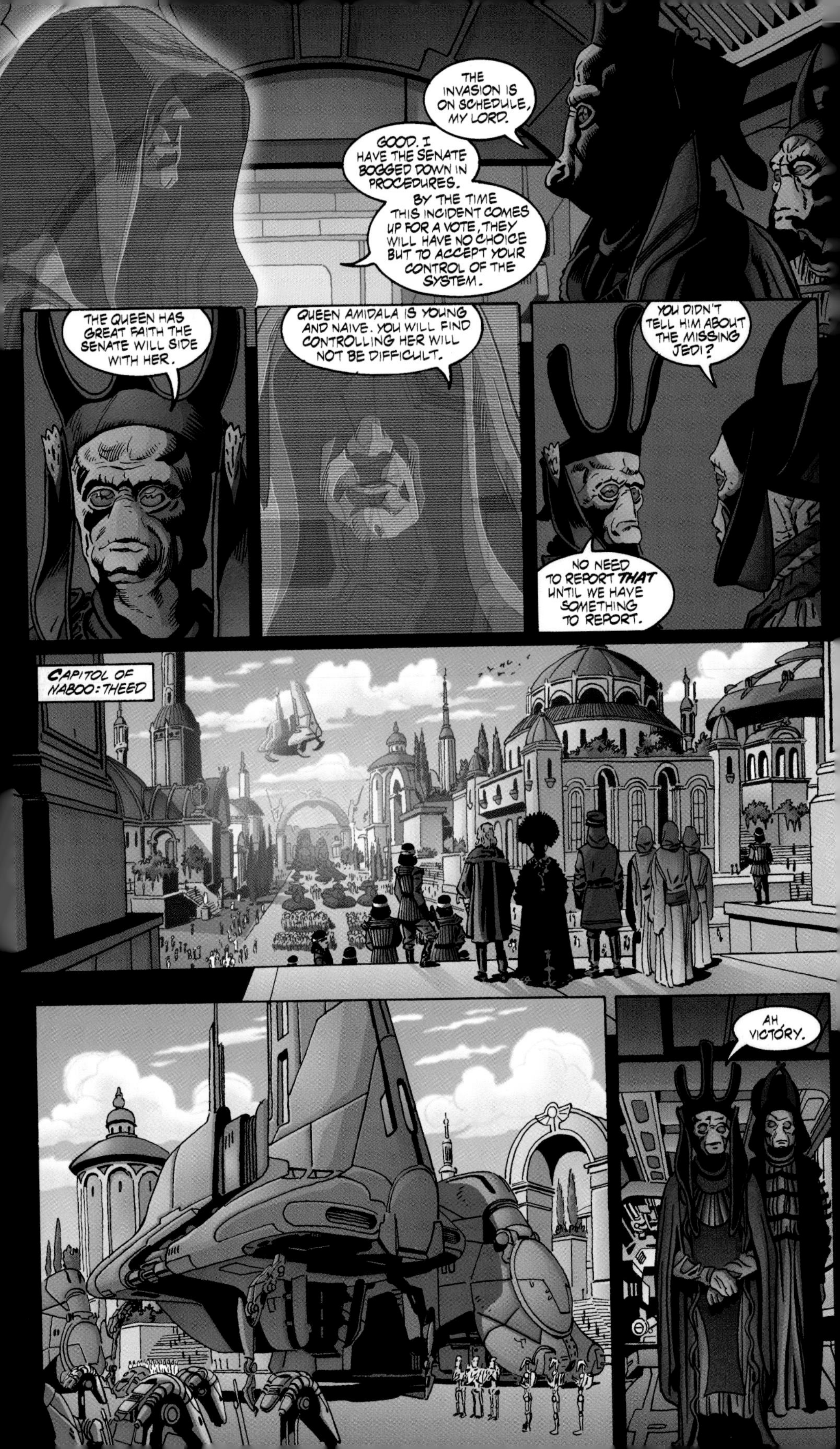
THE INVASION IS ON SCHEDULE, MY LORD.
GOOD. I HAVE THE SENATE BOGGED DOWN IN PROCEDURES.
BY THE TIME THIS INCIDENT COMES UP FOR A VOTE, THEY WILL HAVE NO CHOICE BUT TO ACCEPT YOUR CONTROL OF THE SYSTEM.
THE QUEEN HAS GREAT FAITH THE SENATE WILL SIDE WITH HER.
QUEEN AMIDALA IS YOUNG AND NAIVE. YOU WILL FIND CONTROLLING HER WILL NOT BE DIFFICULT.
YOU DIDN'T TELL HIM ABOUT THE MISSING JEDI?
NO NEED TO REPORT THAT UNTIL WE HAVE SOMETHING TO REPORT.
CAPITOL OF NABOO: THEED
AH VICTORY.

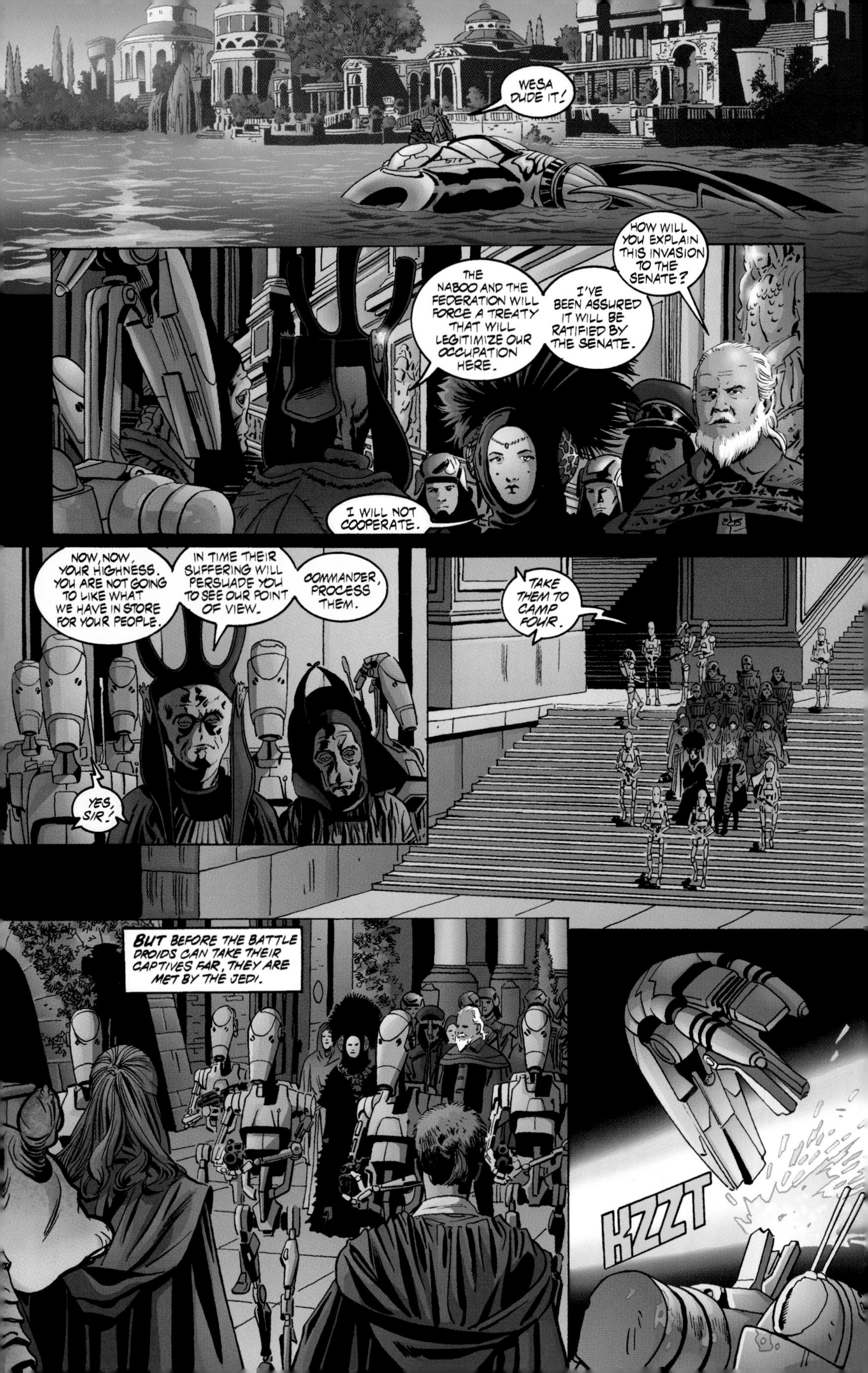
WESA DUDE IT!
HOW WILL YOU EXPLAIN THIS INVASION TO THE SENATE?
THE NABOO AND THE FEDERATION WILL FORCE A TREATY THAT WILL LEGITIMIZE OUR OCCUPATION HERE.
I'VE BEEN ASSURED IT WILL BE RATIFIED BY THE SENATE.
I WILL NOT COOPERATE.
NOW, NOW, YOUR HIGHNESS. YOU ARE NOT GOING TO LIKE WHAT WE HAVE IN STORE FOR YOUR PEOPLE.
IN TIME THEIR SUFFERING WILL PERSUADE YOU TO SEE OUR POINT OF VIEW.
COMMANDER, PROCESS THEM.
YES, SIR!
TAKE THEM TO CAMP FOUR.
BUT BEFORE THE BATTLE DROIDS CAN TAKE THEIR CAPTIVES FAR, THEY ARE MET BY THE JEDI.
HZZT

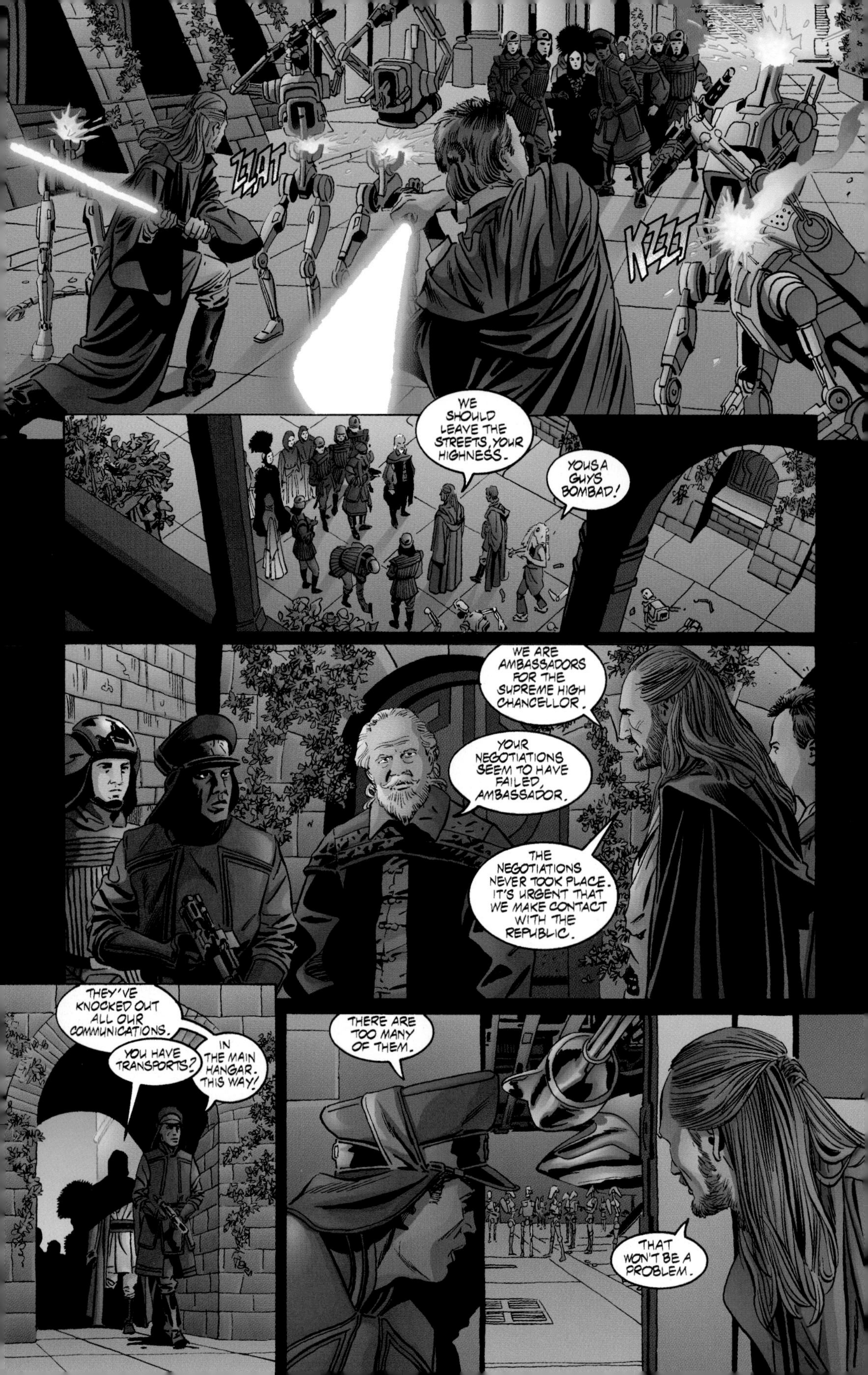
ZZAT
KZEET
WE SHOULD LEAVE THE STREETS, YOUR HIGHNESS.
YOUSA GUYS BOMBAD!
WE ARE AMBASSADORS FOR THE SUPREME HIGH CHANCELLOR.
YOUR NEGOTIATIONS SEEM TO HAVE FAILED, AMBASSADOR.
THE NEGOTIATIONS NEVER TOOK PLACE. IT'S URGENT THAT WE MAKE CONTACT WITH THE REPUBLIC.
THEY'VE KNOCKED OUT ALL OUR COMMUNICATIONS.
YOU HAVE TRANSPORTS?
IN THE MAIN HANGAR. THIS WAY!
THERE ARE TOO MANY OF THEM.
THAT WON'T BE A PROBLEM.

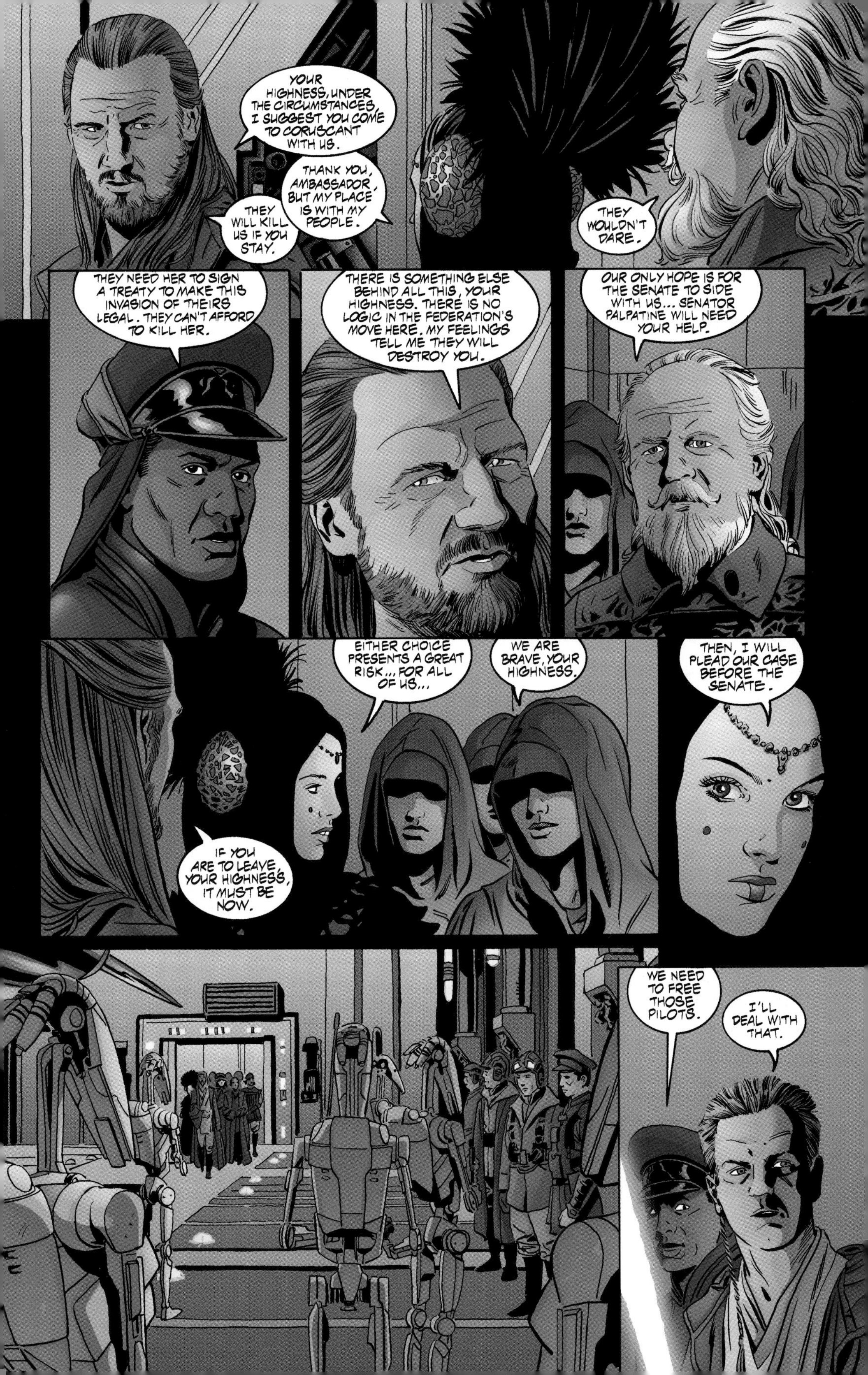
YOUR HIGHNESS, UNDER THE CIRCUMSTANCES, I SUGGEST YOU COME TO CORUSCANT WITH US.
THANK YOU, AMBASSADOR, BUT MY PLACE IS WITH MY PEOPLE.
THEY WILL KILL US IF YOU STAY.
THEY WOULDN'T DARE.
THEY NEED HER TO SIGN A TREATY TO MAKE THIS INVASION OF THEIRS LEGAL. THEY CAN'T AFFORD TO KILL HER.
THERE IS SOMETHING ELSE BEHIND ALL THIS, YOUR HIGHNESS. THERE IS NO LOGIC IN THE FEDERATION'S MOVE HERE. MY FEELINGS TELL ME THEY WILL DESTROY YOU.
OUR ONLY HOPE IS FOR THE SENATE TO SIDE WITH US... SENATOR PALPATINE WILL NEED YOUR HELP.
IF YOU ARE TO LEAVE, YOUR HIGHNESS, IT MUST BE NOW.
EITHER CHOICE PRESENTS A GREAT RISK... FOR ALL OF US...
WE ARE BRAVE, YOUR HIGHNESS.
THEN, I WILL PLEAD OUR CASE BEFORE THE SENATE.
WE NEED TO FREE THOSE PILOTS.
I'LL DEAL WITH THAT.

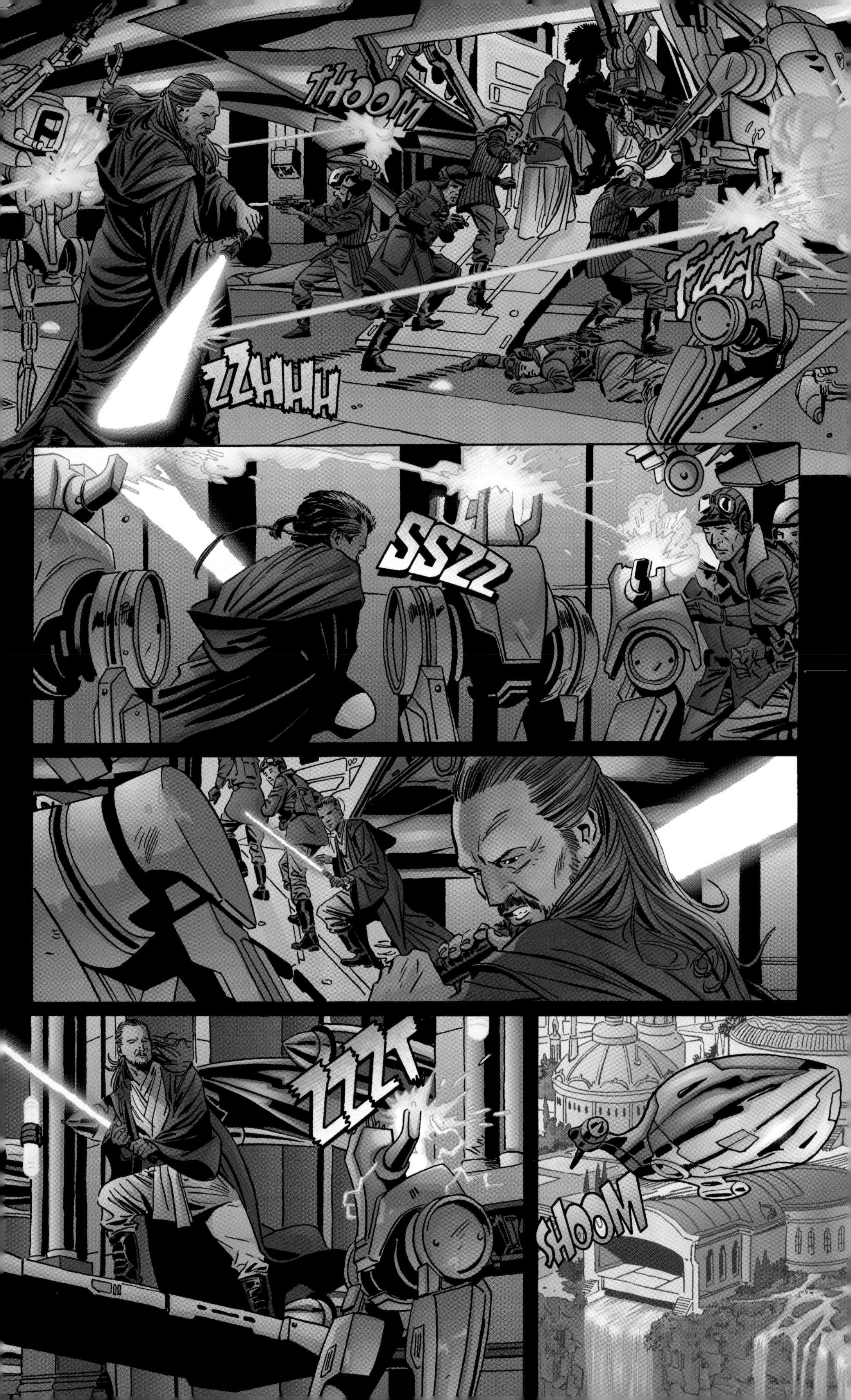
THOOM
FZZT
ZZHHH
SSZZ
ZZZT
SHOOM

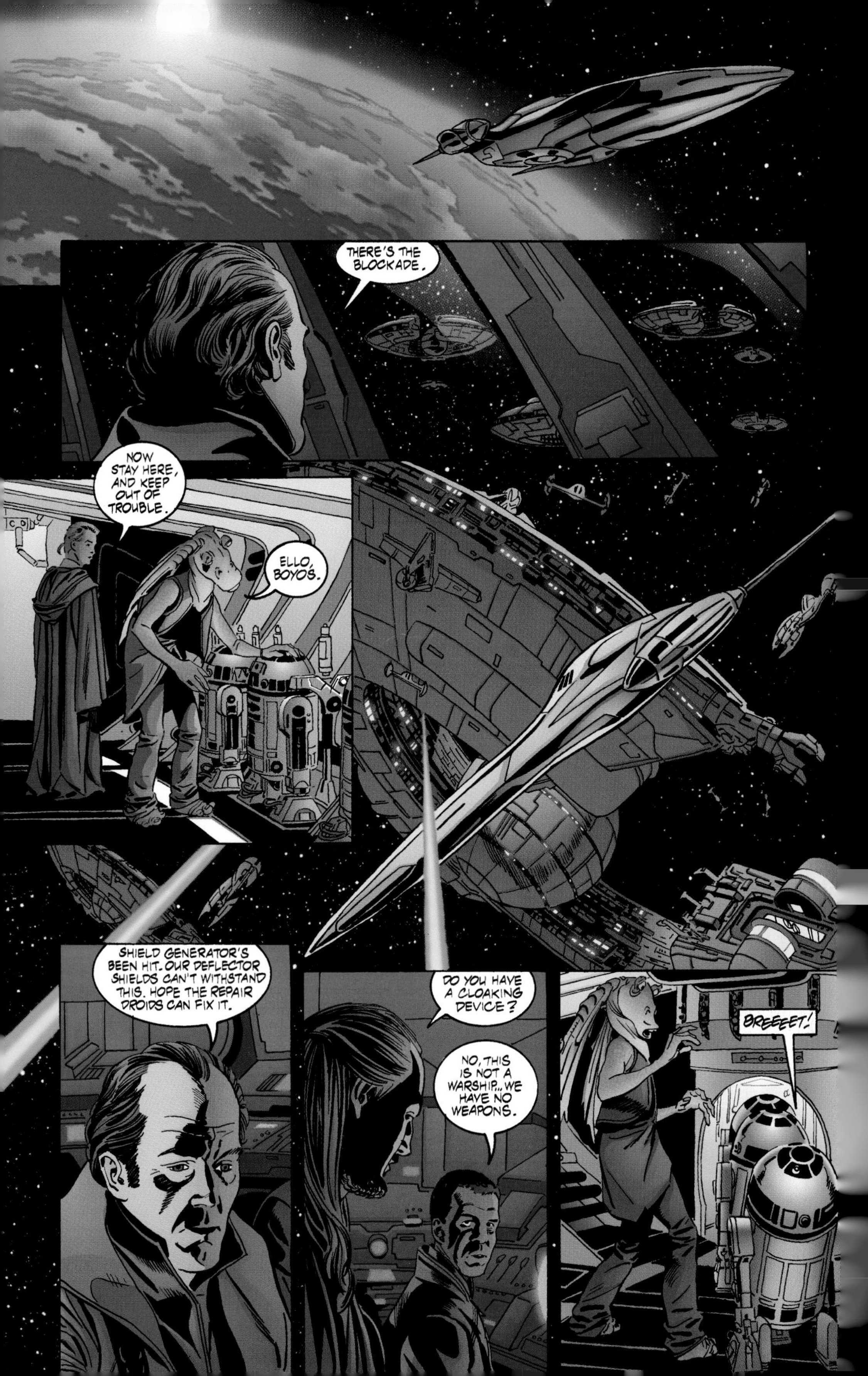
THERE'S THE BLOCKADE.
NOW STAY HERE, AND KEEP OUT OF TROUBLE.
ELLO, BOYOS.
SHIELD GENERATOR'S BEEN HIT. OUR DEFLECTOR SHIELDS CAN'T WITHSTAND THIS. HOPE THE REPAIR DROIDS CAN FIX IT.
DO YOU HAVE A CLOAKING DEVICE?
NO, THIS IS NOT A WARSHIP... WE HAVE NO WEAPONS.
BREEEET!

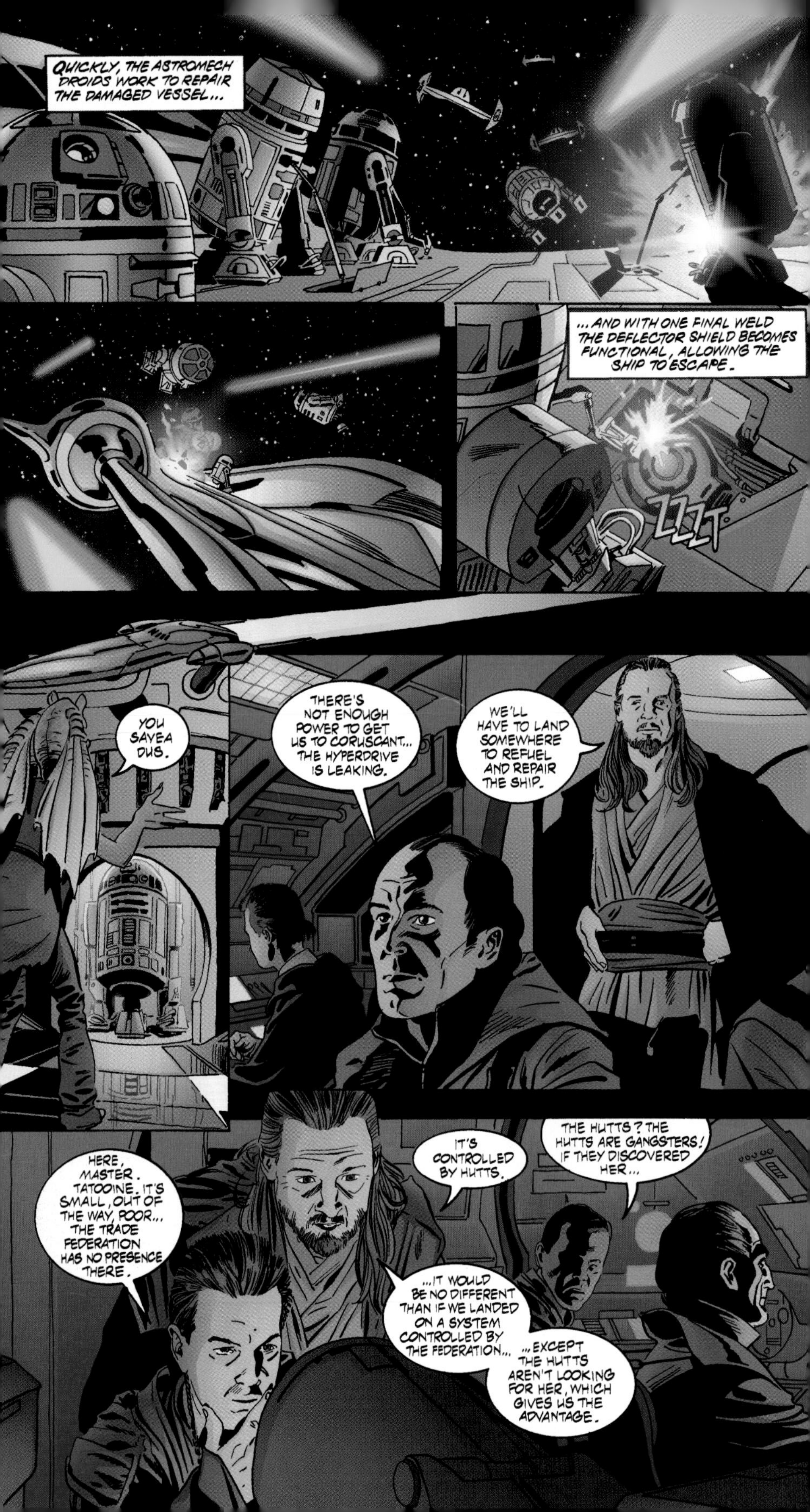
QUICKLY, THE ASTROMECH DROIDS WORK TO REPAIR THE DAMAGED VESSEL...
...AND WITH ONE FINAL WELD THE DEFLECTOR SHIELD BECOMES FUNCTIONAL, ALLOWING THE SHIP TO ESCAPE.
ZZZT
YOU SAVEA DUS.
THERE'S NOT ENOUGH POWER TO GET US TO CORUSCANT... THE HYPERDRIVE IS LEAKING.
WE'LL HAVE TO LAND SOMEWHERE TO REFUEL AND REPAIR THE SHIP.
HERE, MASTER. TATOOINE. IT'S SMALL, OUT OF THE WAY, POOR... THE TRADE FEDERATION HAS NO PRESENCE THERE.
IT'S CONTROLLED BY HUTTS.
THE HUTTS? THE HUTTS ARE GANGSTERS! IF THEY DISCOVERED HER...
...IT WOULD BE NO DIFFERENT THAN IF WE LANDED ON A SYSTEM CONTROLLED BY THE FEDERATION...
...EXCEPT THE HUTTS AREN'T LOOKING FOR HER, WHICH GIVES US THE ADVANTAGE.

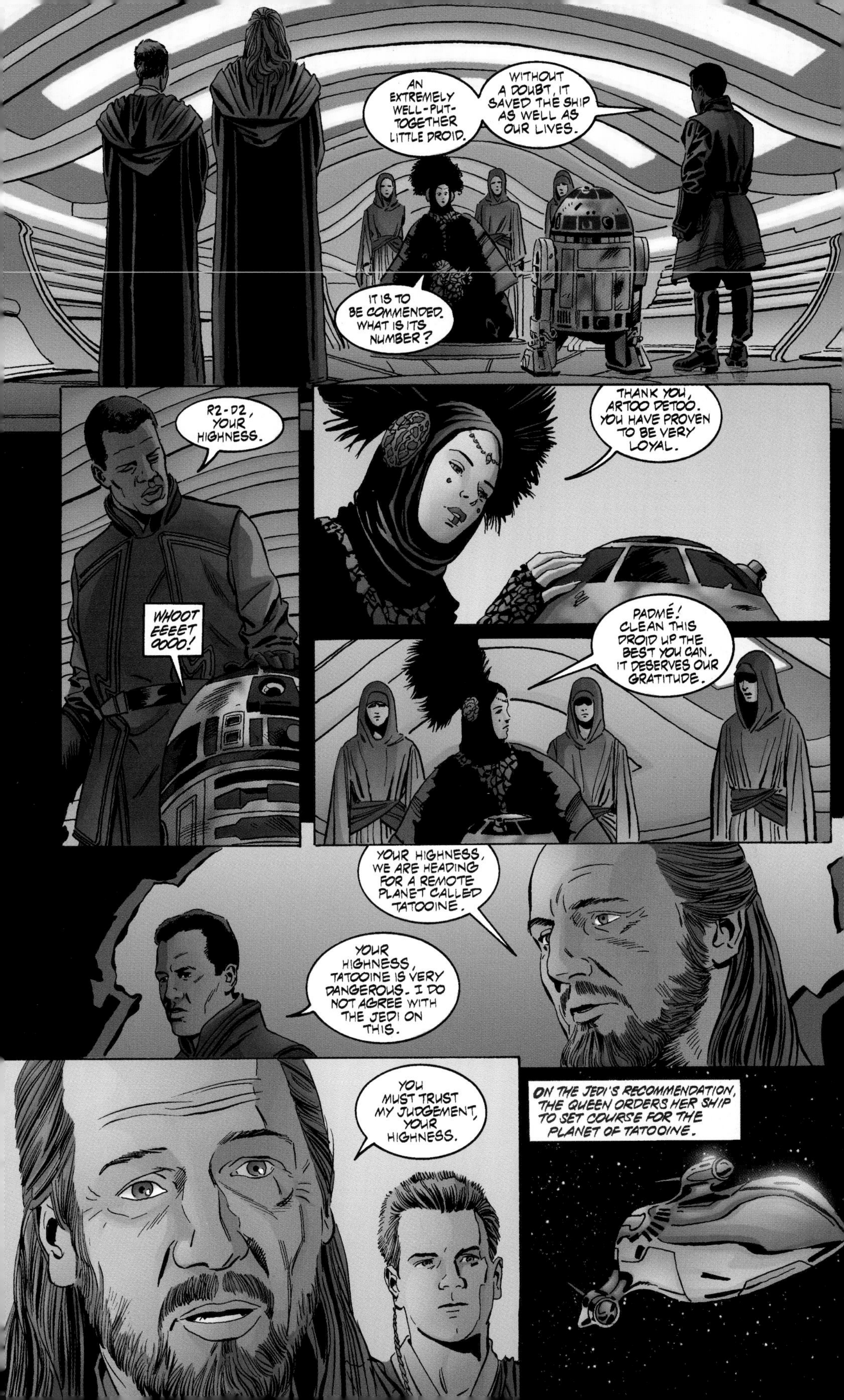
AN EXTREMELY WELL-PUT-TOGETHER LITTLE DROID.
WITHOUT A DOUBT, IT SAVED THE SHIP AS WELL AS OUR LIVES.
IT IS TO BE COMMENDED. WHAT IS ITS NUMBER?
R2-D2, YOUR HIGHNESS.
WHOOT EEEET OOOO!
THANK YOU, ARTOO DETOO. YOU HAVE PROVEN TO BE VERY LOYAL.
PADMÉ! CLEAN THIS DROID UP THE BEST YOU CAN. IT DESERVES OUR GRATITUDE.
YOUR HIGHNESS, WE ARE HEADING FOR A REMOTE PLANET CALLED TATOOINE.
YOUR HIGHNESS, TATOOINE IS VERY DANGEROUS. I DO NOT AGREE WITH THE JEDI ON THIS.
YOU MUST TRUST MY JUDGEMENT, YOUR HIGHNESS.
ON THE JEDI'S RECOMMENDATION, THE QUEEN ORDERS HER SHIP TO SET COURSE FOR THE PLANET OF TATOOINE.

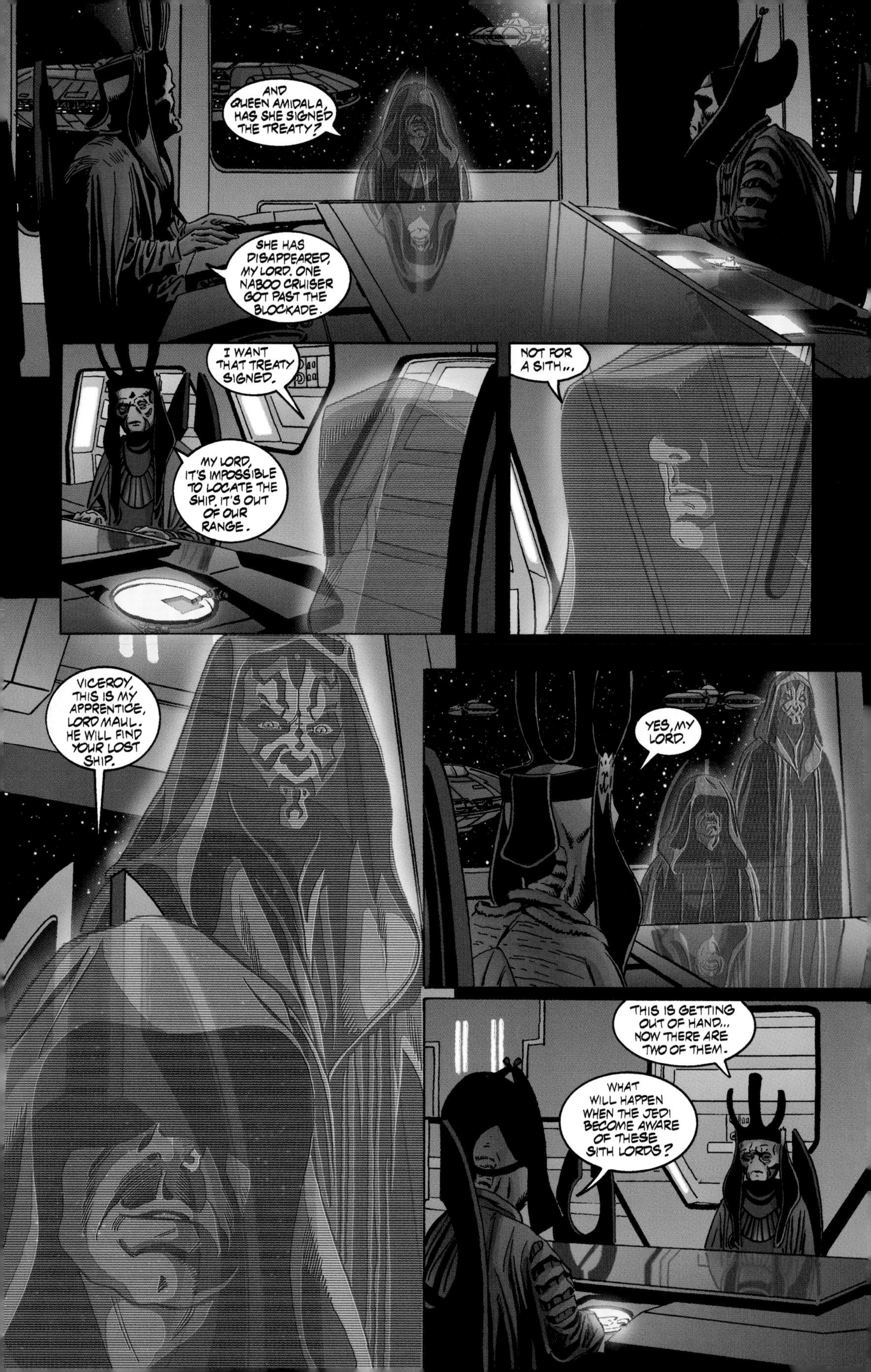
AND QUEEN AMIDALA, HAS SHE SIGNED THE TREATY?
SHE HAS DISAPPEARED, MY LORD. ONE NABOO CRUISER GOT PAST THE BLOCKADE.
I WANT THAT TREATY SIGNED.
MY LORD, IT'S IMPOSSIBLE TO LOCATE THE SHIP. IT'S OUT OF OUR RANGE.
NOT FOR A SITH...
VICEROY, THIS IS MY APPRENTICE, LORD MAUL. HE WILL FIND YOUR LOST SHIP.
YES, MY LORD.
THIS IS GETTING OUT OF HAND... NOW THERE ARE TWO OF THEM.
WHAT WILL HAPPEN WHEN THE JEDI BECOME AWARE OF THESE SITH LORDS?

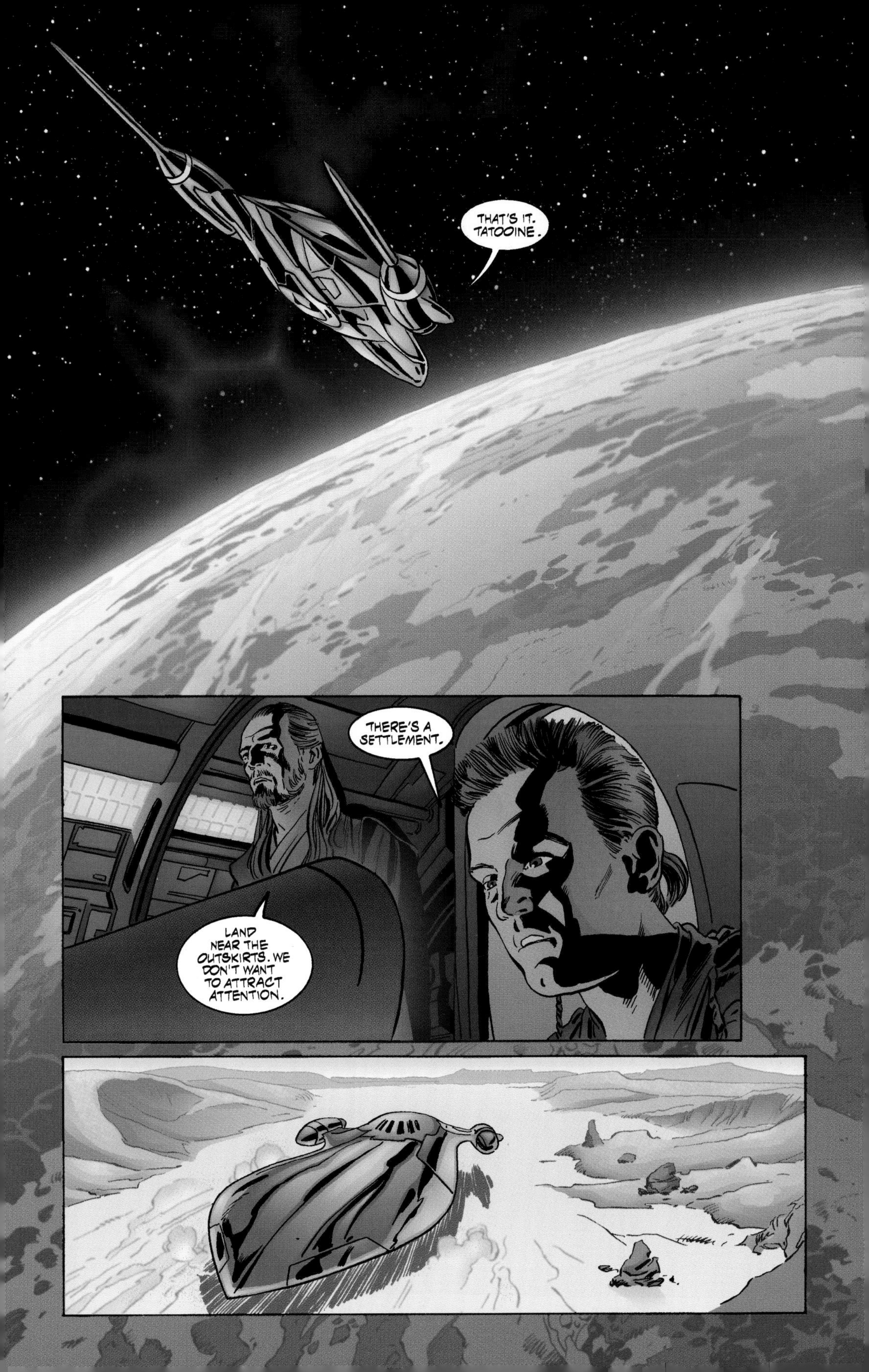
THAT'S IT. TATOOINE.
THERE'S A SETTLEMENT.
LAND NEAR THE OUTSKIRTS. WE DON'T WANT TO ATTRACT ATTENTION.

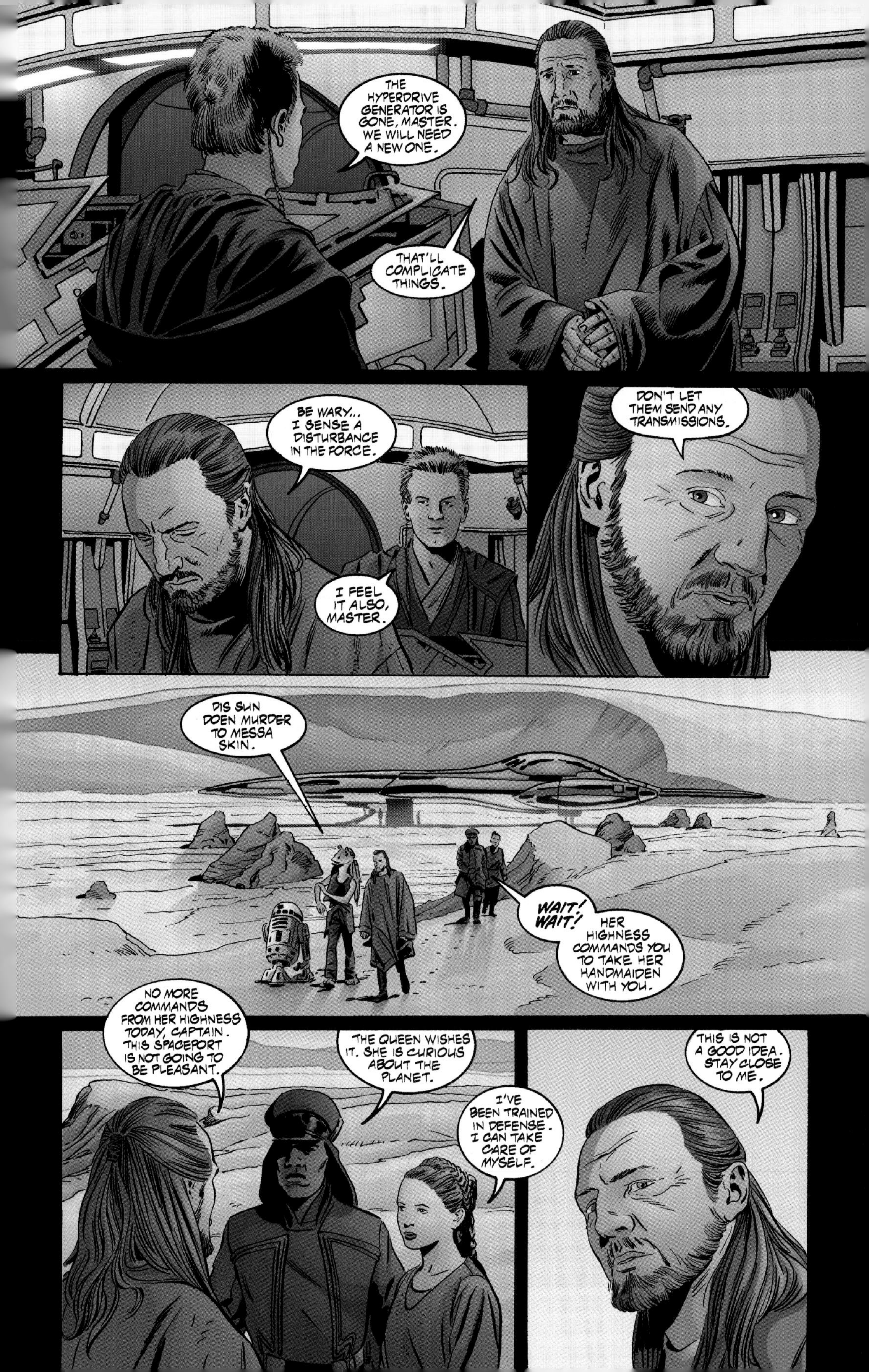
THE HYPERDRIVE GENERATOR IS GONE, MASTER. WE WILL NEED A NEW ONE.
THAT'LL COMPLICATE THINGS.
BE WARY... I SENSE A DISTURBANCE IN THE FORCE.
I FEEL IT ALSO, MASTER.
DON'T LET THEM SEND ANY TRANSMISSIONS.
DIS SUN DOEN MURDER TO MESSA SKIN.
WAIT! WAIT! HER HIGHNESS COMMANDS YOU TO TAKE HER HANDMAIDEN WITH YOU.
NO MORE COMMANDS FROM HER HIGHNESS TODAY, CAPTAIN. THIS SPACEPORT IS NOT GOING TO BE PLEASANT.
THE QUEEN WISHES IT. SHE IS CURIOUS ABOUT THE PLANET.
I'VE BEEN TRAINED IN DEFENSE. I CAN TAKE CARE OF MYSELF.
THIS IS NOT A GOOD IDEA. STAY CLOSE TO ME.

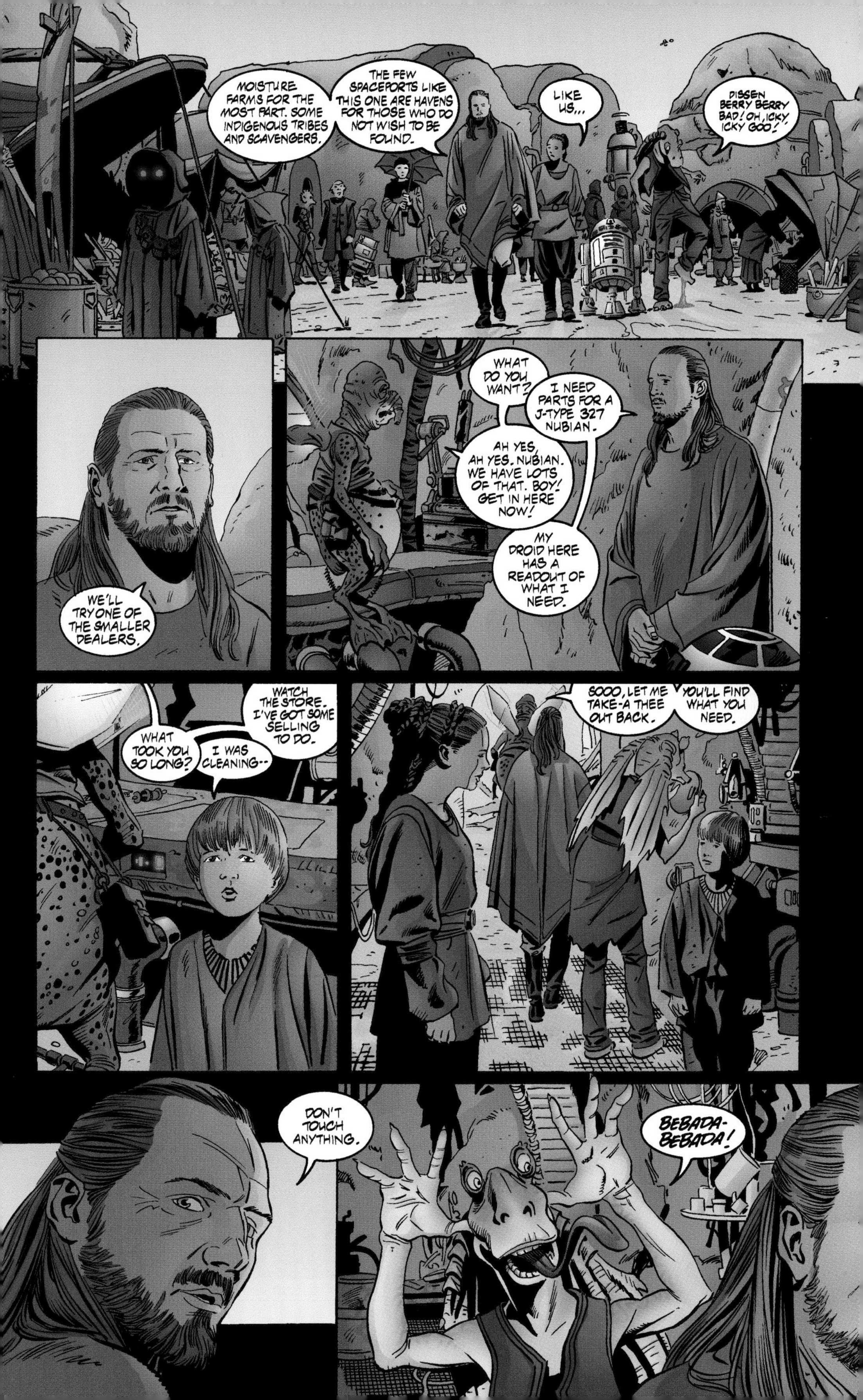
MOISTURE FARMS FOR THE MOST PART. SOME INDIGENOUS TRIBES AND SCAVENGERS.
THE FEW SPACEPORTS LIKE THIS ONE ARE HAVENS FOR THOSE WHO DO NOT WISH TO BE FOUND.
LIKE US...
DISSEN BERRY BERRY BAD! OH, ICKY, ICKY GOO!
WE'LL TRY ONE OF THE SMALLER DEALERS.
WHAT DO YOU WANT?
I NEED PARTS FOR A J-TYPE 327 NUBIAN.
AH YES, AH YES. NUBIAN. WE HAVE LOTS OF THAT. BOY! GET IN HERE NOW!
MY DROID HERE HAS A READOUT OF WHAT I NEED.
WHAT TOOK YOU SO LONG?
I WAS CLEANING--
WATCH THE STORE. I'VE GOT SOME SELLING TO DO.
SOOO, LET ME TAKE-A THEE OUT BACK.
YOU'LL FIND WHAT YOU NEED.
DON'T TOUCH ANYTHING.
BEBADA-BEBADA!

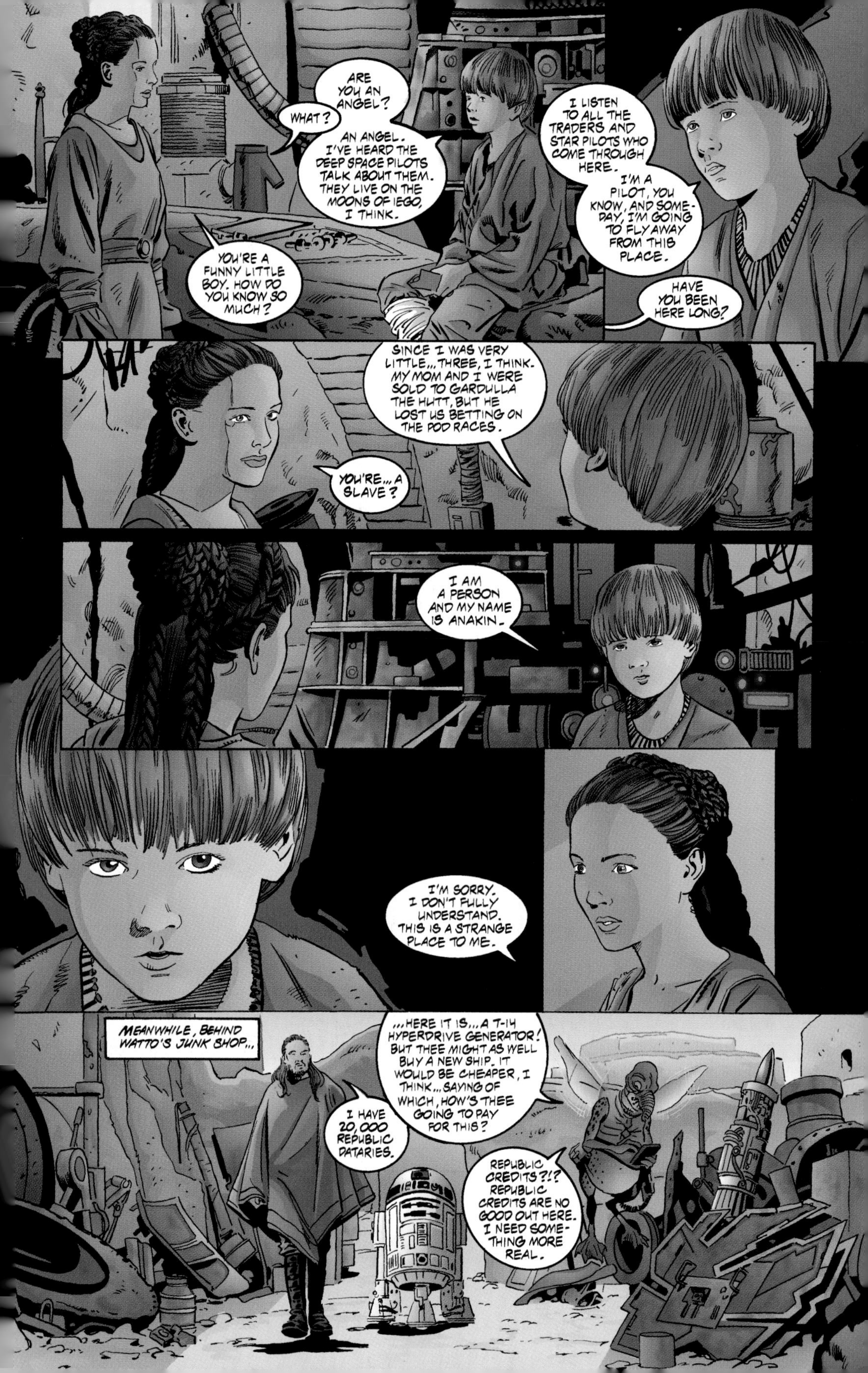
ARE YOU AN ANGEL?
WHAT?
AN ANGEL. I'VE HEARD THE DEEP SPACE PILOTS TALK ABOUT THEM. THEY LIVE ON THE MOONS OF IEGO, I THINK.
YOU'RE A FUNNY LITTLE BOY. HOW DO YOU KNOW SO MUCH?
I LISTEN TO ALL THE TRADERS AND STAR PILOTS WHO COME THROUGH HERE.
I'M A PILOT, YOU KNOW, AND SOMEDAY, I'M GOING TO FLY AWAY FROM THIS PLACE.
HAVE YOU BEEN HERE LONG?
SINCE I WAS VERY LITTLE... THREE, I THINK. MY MOM AND I WERE SOLD TO GARDULLA THE HUTT, BUT HE LOST US BETTING ON THE POD RACES.
YOU'RE... A SLAVE?
I AM A PERSON AND MY NAME IS ANAKIN.
I'M SORRY. I DON'T FULLY UNDERSTAND. THIS IS A STRANGE PLACE TO ME.
MEANWHILE, BEHIND WATTO'S JUNK SHOP...
...HERE IT IS... A T-14 HYPERDRIVE GENERATOR! BUT THEE MIGHT AS WELL BUY A NEW SHIP. IT WOULD BE CHEAPER, I THINK... SAYING OF WHICH, HOW'S THEE GOING TO PAY FOR THIS?
I HAVE 20,000 REPUBLIC DATARIES.
REPUBLIC CREDITS?!? REPUBLIC CREDITS ARE NO GOOD OUT HERE. I NEED SOMETHING MORE REAL.

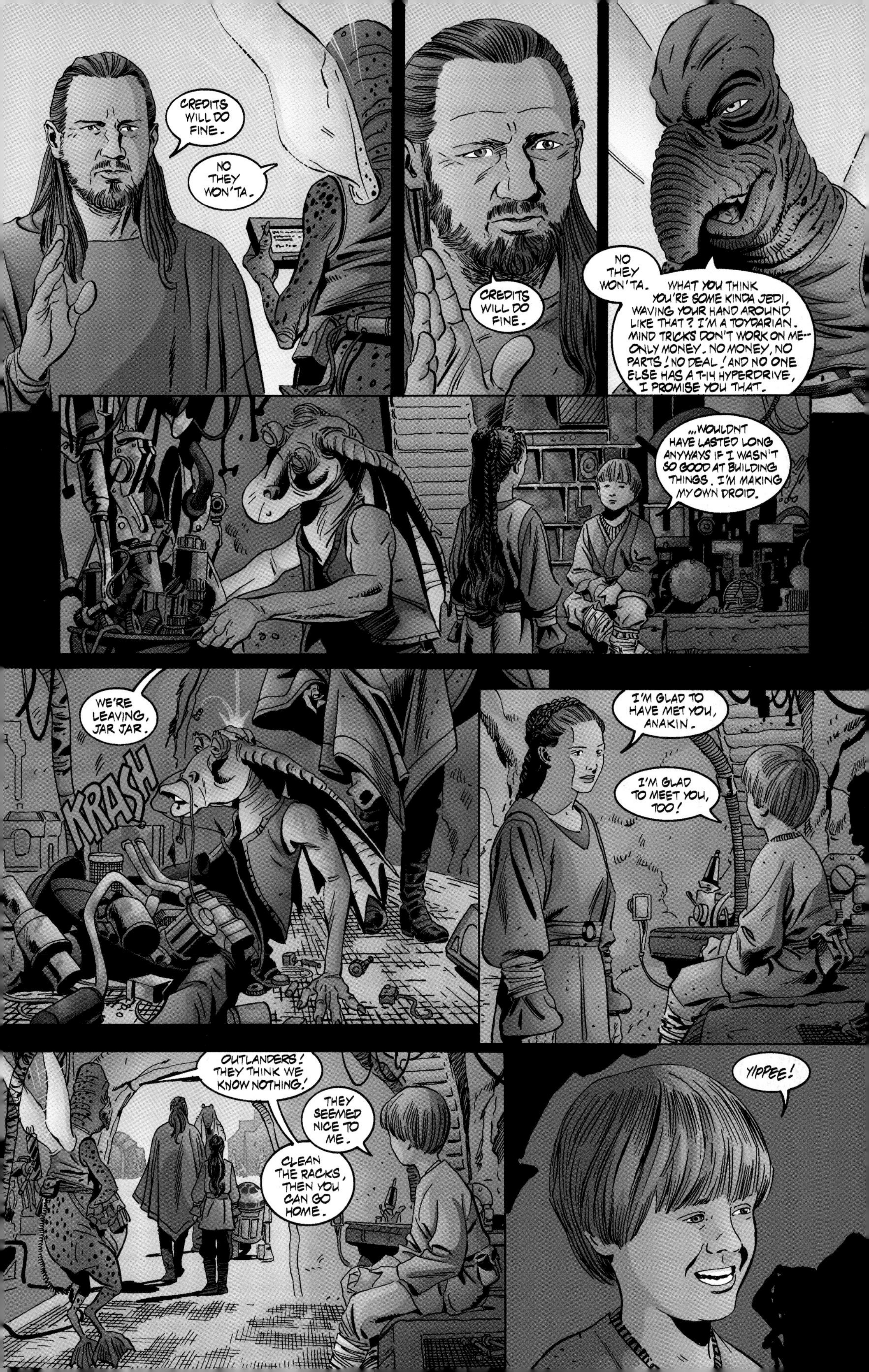
CREDITS WILL DO FINE.
NO THEY WON'TA.
CREDITS WILL DO FINE.
NO THEY WON'TA.
WHAT YOU THINK YOU'RE SOME KINDA JEDI, WAVING YOUR HAND AROUND LIKE THAT? I'M A TOYDARIAN. MIND TRICKS DON'T WORK ON ME-- ONLY MONEY. NO MONEY, NO PARTS! NO DEAL! AND NO ONE ELSE HAS A T-14 HYPERDRIVE, I PROMISE YOU THAT.
...WOULDNT HAVE LASTED LONG ANYWAYS IF I WASN'T SO GOOD AT BUILDING THINGS. I'M MAKING MY OWN DROID.
WE'RE LEAVING, JAR JAR.
KRASH
I'M GLAD TO HAVE MET YOU, ANAKIN.
I'M GLAD TO MEET YOU, TOO!
OUTLANDERS! THEY THINK WE KNOW NOTHING!
THEY SEEMED NICE TO ME.
CLEAN THE RACKS, THEN YOU CAN GO HOME.
YIPPEE!

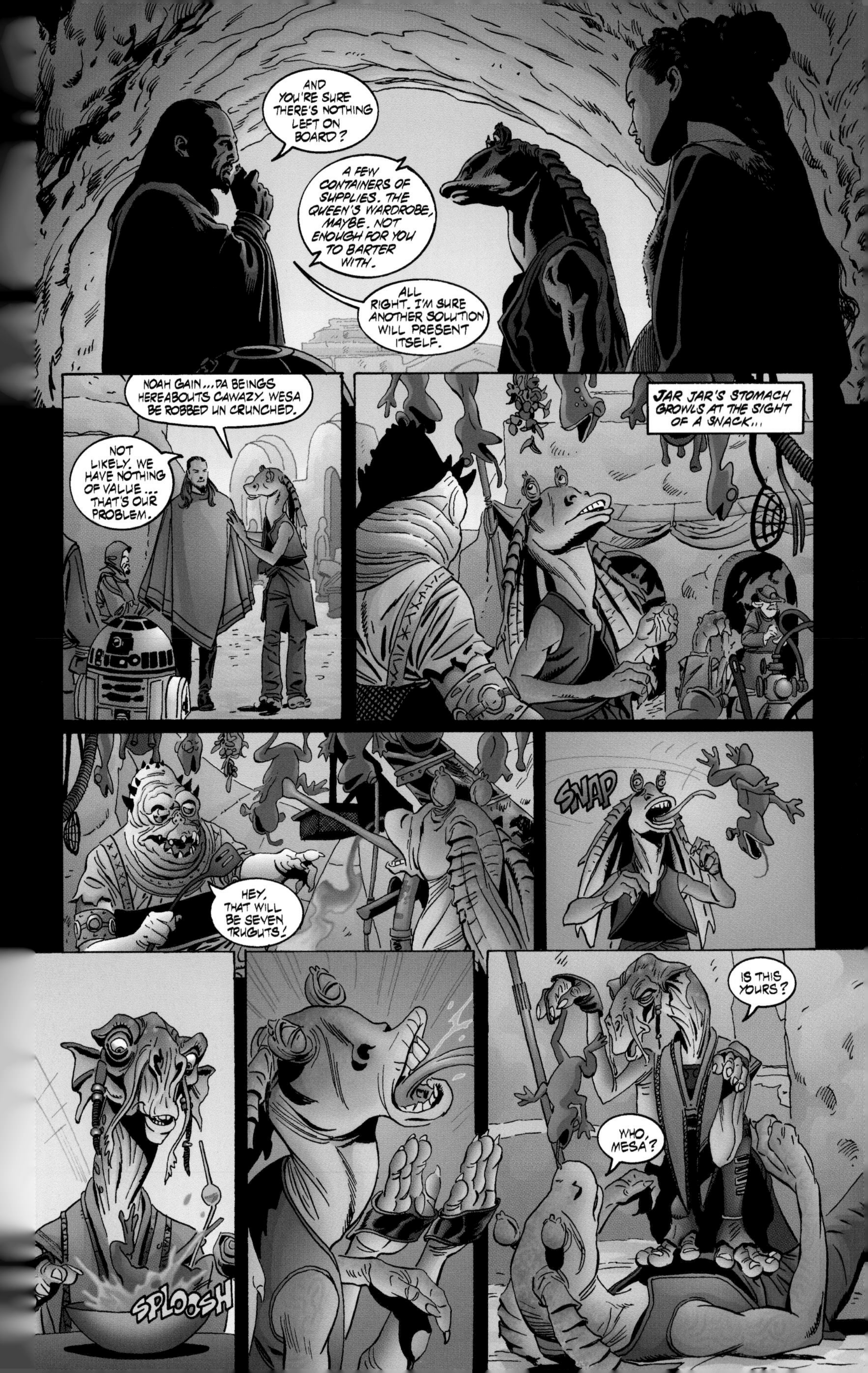
AND YOU'RE SURE THERE'S NOTHING LEFT ON BOARD?
A FEW CONTAINERS OF SUPPLIES. THE QUEEN'S WARDROBE, MAYBE. NOT ENOUGH FOR YOU TO BARTER WITH.
ALL RIGHT. I'M SURE ANOTHER SOLUTION WILL PRESENT ITSELF.
NOAH GAIN...DA BEINGS HEREABOUTS CAWAZY. WESA BE ROBBED UN CRUNCHED.
NOT LIKELY. WE HAVE NOTHING OF VALUE... THAT'S OUR PROBLEM.
JAR JAR'S STOMACH GROWLS AT THE SIGHT OF A SNACK...
HEY, THAT WILL BE SEVEN TRUGUTS!
SNAP
SPLOOSH
IS THIS YOURS?
WHO, MESA?

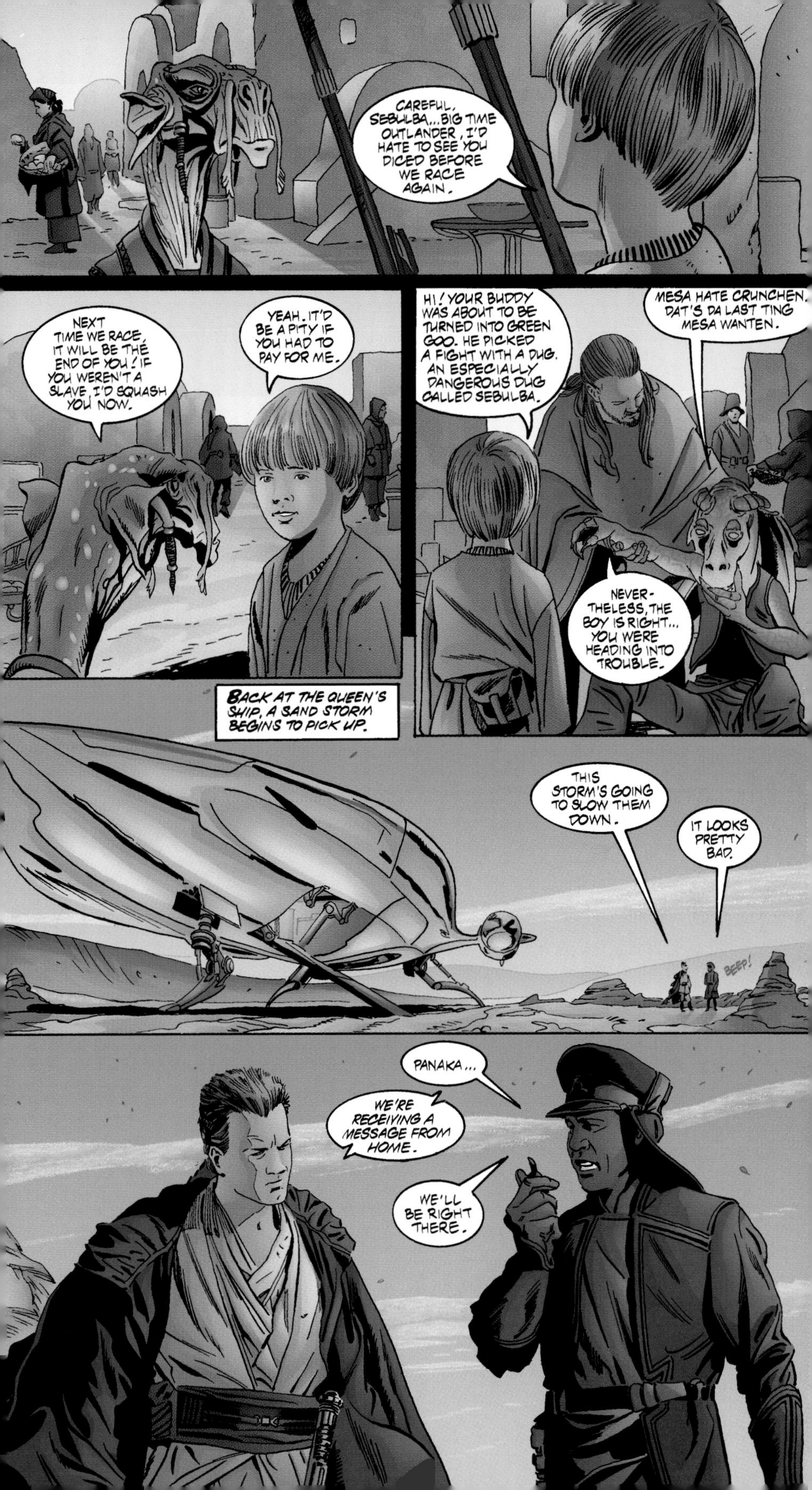
CAREFUL, SEBULBA... BIG TIME OUTLANDER, I'D HATE TO SEE YOU DICED BEFORE WE RACE AGAIN.
NEXT TIME WE RACE, IT WILL BE THE END OF YOU! IF YOU WEREN'T A SLAVE, I'D SQUASH YOU NOW.
YEAH. IT'D BE A PITY IF YOU HAD TO PAY FOR ME.
HI! YOUR BUDDY WAS ABOUT TO BE TURNED INTO GREEN GOO. HE PICKED A FIGHT WITH A DUG. AN ESPECIALLY DANGEROUS DUG CALLED SEBULBA.
MESA HATE CRUNCHEN. DAT'S DA LAST TING MESA WANTEN.
NEVER-THELESS, THE BOY IS RIGHT... YOU WERE HEADING INTO TROUBLE.
BACK AT THE QUEEN'S SHIP, A SAND STORM BEGINS TO PICK UP.
THIS STORM'S GOING TO SLOW THEM DOWN.
IT LOOKS PRETTY BAD.
BEEP!
PANAKA...
WE'RE RECEIVING A MESSAGE FROM HOME.
WE'LL BE RIGHT THERE.

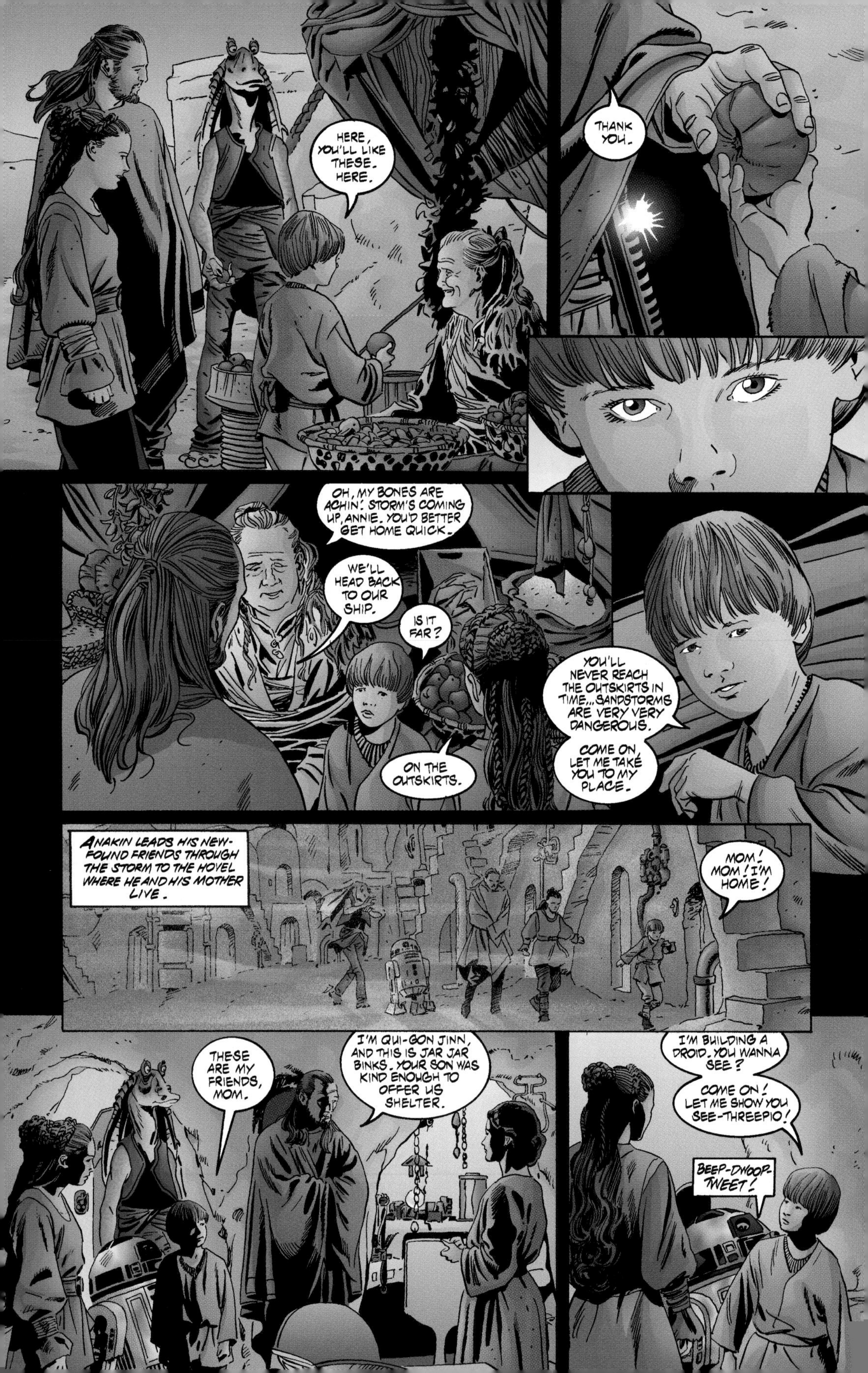
HERE, YOU'LL LIKE THESE. HERE.
THANK YOU.
OH, MY BONES ARE ACHIN'. STORM'S COMING UP, ANNIE. YOU'D BETTER GET HOME QUICK.
WE'LL HEAD BACK TO OUR SHIP.
IS IT FAR?
ON THE OUTSKIRTS.
YOU'LL NEVER REACH THE OUTSKIRTS IN TIME... SANDSTORMS ARE VERY VERY DANGEROUS.
COME ON LET ME TAKE YOU TO MY PLACE.
ANAKIN LEADS HIS NEW-FOUND FRIENDS THROUGH THE STORM TO THE HOVEL WHERE HE AND HIS MOTHER LIVE.
MOM! MOM! I'M HOME!
THESE ARE MY FRIENDS, MOM.
I'M QUI-GON JINN, AND THIS IS JAR JAR BINKS. YOUR SON WAS KIND ENOUGH TO OFFER US SHELTER.
I'M BUILDING A DROID. YOU WANNA SEE?
COME ON! LET ME SHOW YOU SEE-THREEPIO!
BEEP-DWOOP-TWEET!

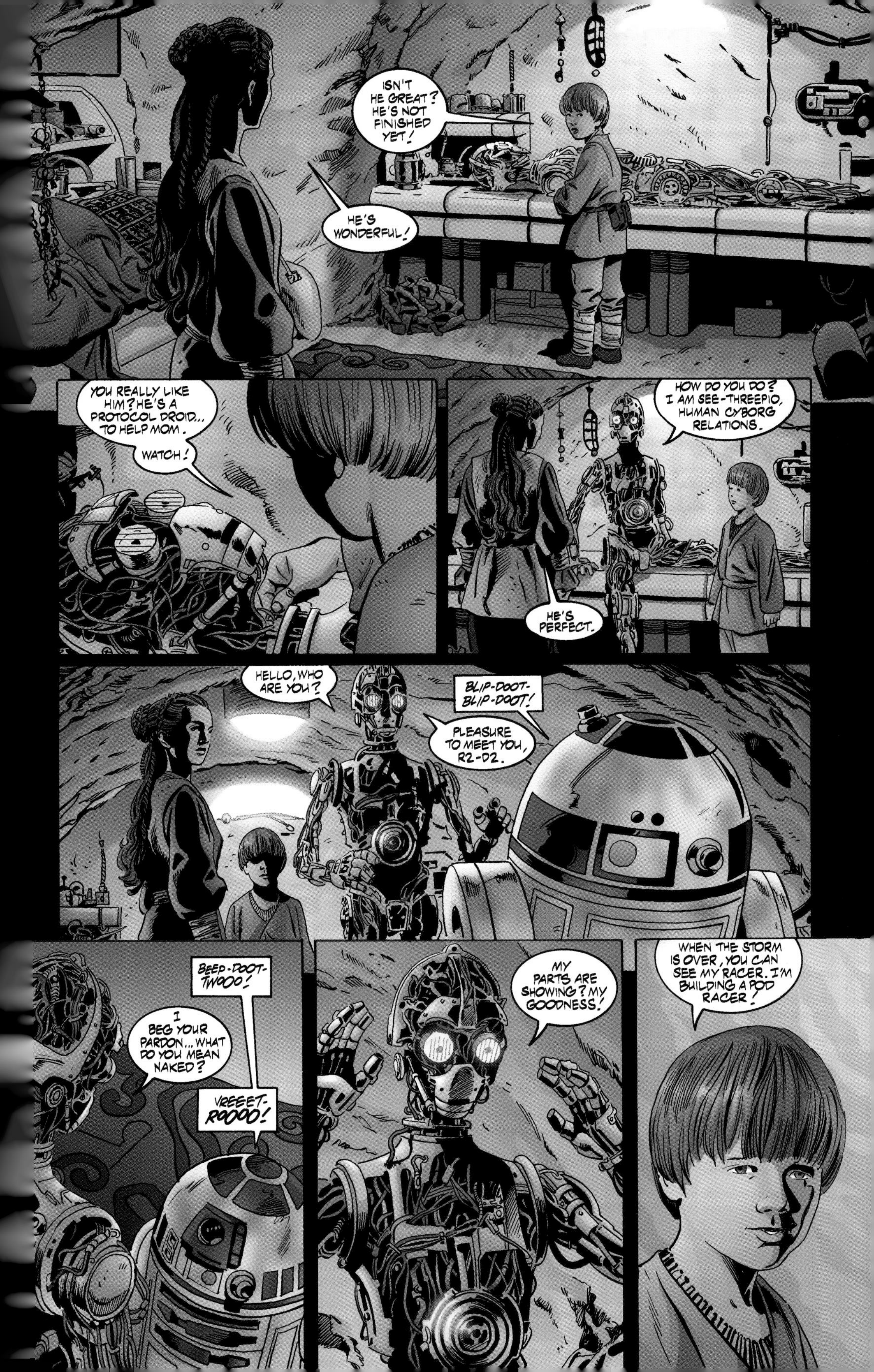
ISN'T HE GREAT? HE'S NOT FINISHED YET!
HE'S WONDERFUL!
YOU REALLY LIKE HIM? HE'S A PROTOCOL DROID... TO HELP MOM.
WATCH!
HOW DO YOU DO? I AM SEE-THREEPIO, HUMAN CYBORG RELATIONS.
HE'S PERFECT.
HELLO, WHO ARE YOU?
BLIP-DOOT-BLIP-DOOT!
PLEASURE TO MEET YOU, R2-D2.
BEEP-DOOT-TWOOO!
I BEG YOUR PARDON... WHAT DO YOU MEAN NAKED?
VREEET-ROOOO!
MY PARTS ARE SHOWING? MY GOODNESS!
WHEN THE STORM IS OVER, YOU CAN SEE MY RACER. I'M BUILDING A POD RACER!

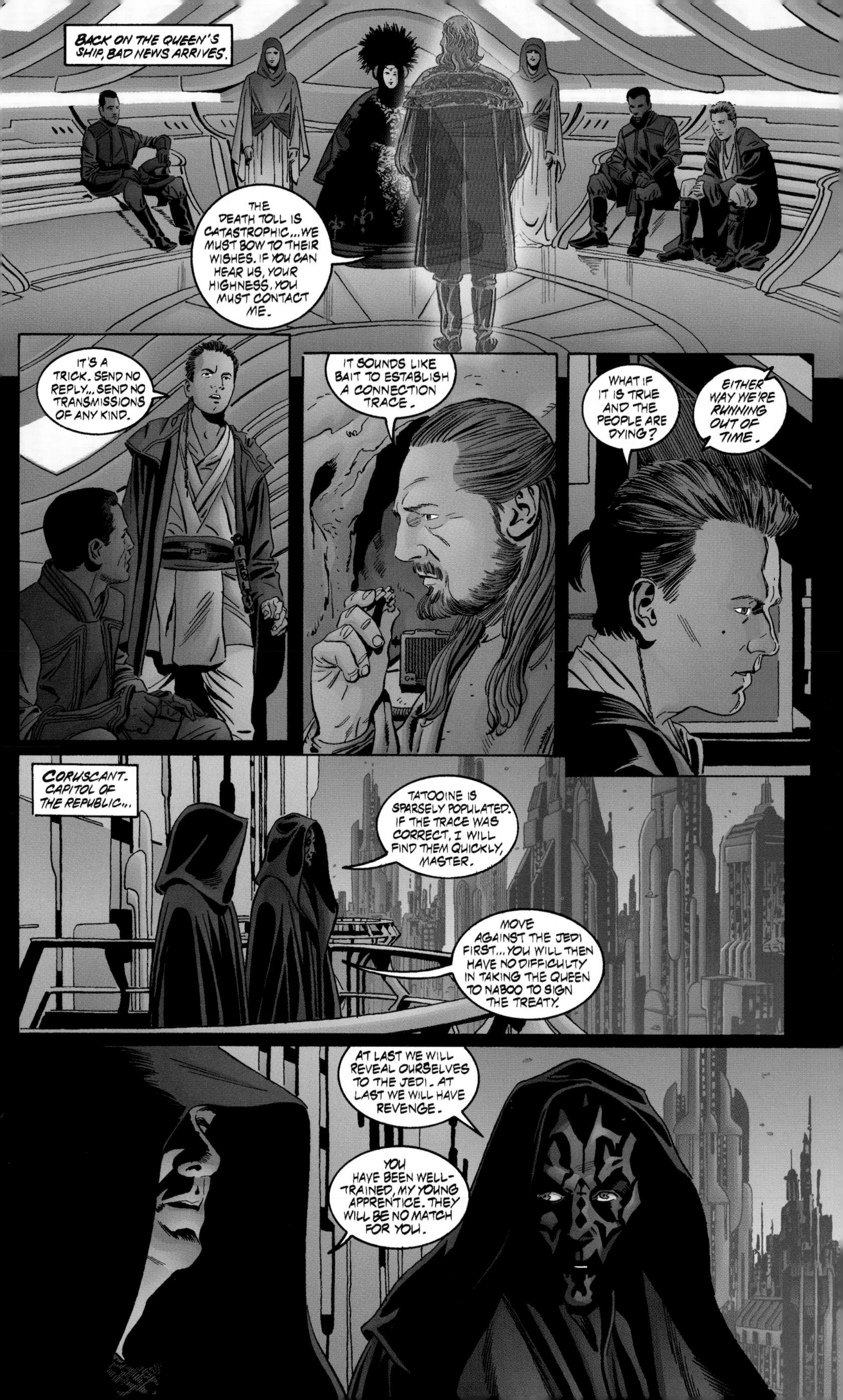
BACK ON THE QUEEN'S SHIP, BAD NEWS ARRIVES.
THE DEATH TOLL IS CATASTROPHIC... WE MUST BOW TO THEIR WISHES. IF YOU CAN HEAR US, YOUR HIGHNESS, YOU MUST CONTACT ME.
IT'S A TRICK. SEND NO REPLY... SEND NO TRANSMISSIONS OF ANY KIND.
IT SOUNDS LIKE BAIT TO ESTABLISH A CONNECTION TRACE.
WHAT IF IT IS TRUE AND THE PEOPLE ARE DYING?
EITHER WAY WE'RE RUNNING OUT OF TIME.
CORUSCANT. CAPITOL OF THE REPUBLIC...
TATOOINE IS SPARSELY POPULATED. IF THE TRACE WAS CORRECT, I WILL FIND THEM QUICKLY, MASTER.
MOVE AGAINST THE JEDI FIRST... YOU WILL THEN HAVE NO DIFFICULTY IN TAKING THE QUEEN TO NABOO TO SIGN THE TREATY.
AT LAST WE WILL REVEAL OURSELVES TO THE JEDI. AT LAST WE WILL HAVE REVENGE.
YOU HAVE BEEN WELL-TRAINED, MY YOUNG APPRENTICE. THEY WILL BE NO MATCH FOR YOU.

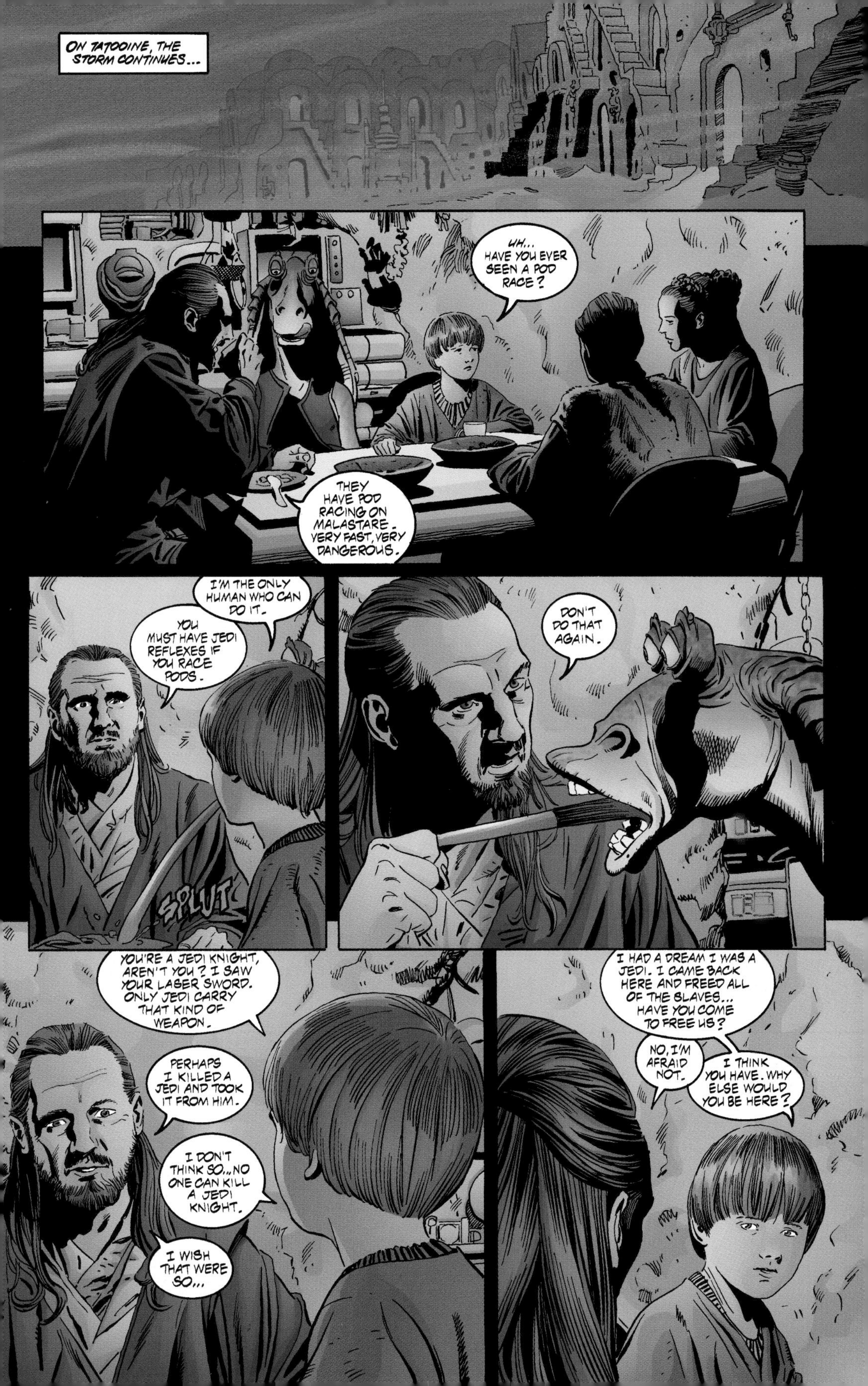

ON TATOOINE, THE STORM CONTINUES...
UH... HAVE YOU EVER SEEN A POD RACE?
THEY HAVE POD RACING ON MALASTARE. VERY FAST, VERY DANGEROUS.
I'M THE ONLY HUMAN WHO CAN DO IT.
YOU MUST HAVE JEDI REFLEXES IF YOU RACE PODS.
SPLUT
DON'T DO THAT AGAIN.
YOU'RE A JEDI KNIGHT, AREN'T YOU? I SAW YOUR LASER SWORD. ONLY JEDI CARRY THAT KIND OF WEAPON.
PERHAPS I KILLED A JEDI AND TOOK IT FROM HIM.
I DON'T THINK SO... NO ONE CAN KILL A JEDI KNIGHT.
I WISH THAT WERE SO...
I HAD A DREAM I WAS A JEDI. I CAME BACK HERE AND FREED ALL OF THE SLAVES... HAVE YOU COME TO FREE US?
NO, I'M AFRAID NOT.
I THINK YOU HAVE. WHY ELSE WOULD YOU BE HERE?

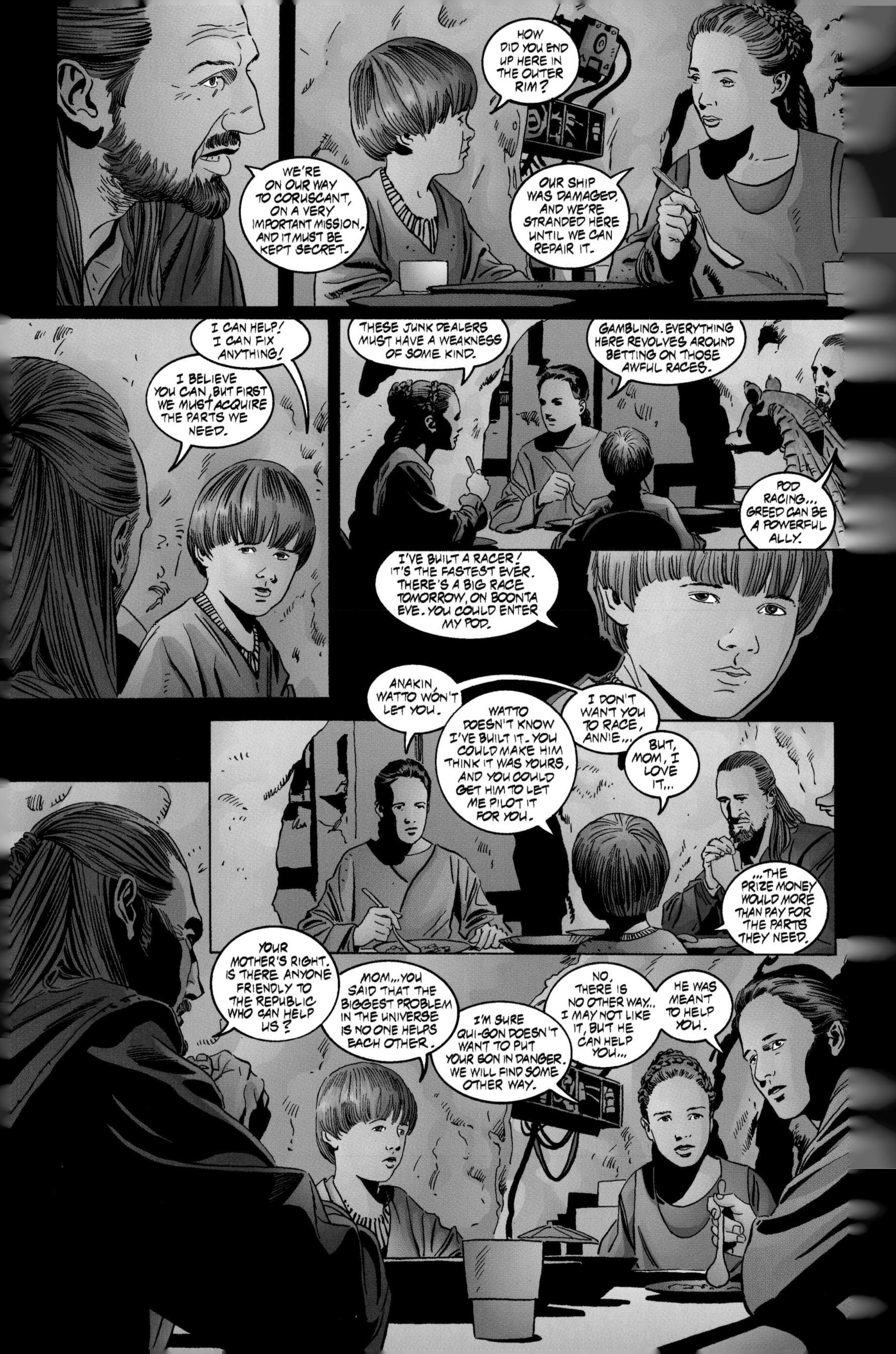
HOW DID YOU END UP HERE IN THE OUTER RIM?
WE'RE ON OUR WAY TO CORUSCANT, ON A VERY IMPORTANT MISSION, AND IT MUST BE KEPT SECRET.
OUR SHIP WAS DAMAGED, AND WE'RE STRANDED HERE UNTIL WE CAN REPAIR IT.
I CAN HELP! I CAN FIX ANYTHING!
I BELIEVE YOU CAN, BUT FIRST WE MUST ACQUIRE THE PARTS WE NEED.
THESE JUNK DEALERS MUST HAVE A WEAKNESS OF SOME KIND.
GAMBLING. EVERYTHING HERE REVOLVES AROUND BETTING ON THOSE AWFUL RACES.
POD RACING... GREED CAN BE A POWERFUL ALLY.
I'VE BUILT A RACER! IT'S THE FASTEST EVER. THERE'S A BIG RACE TOMORROW, ON BOONTA EVE. YOU COULD ENTER MY POD.
ANAKIN, WATTO WON'T LET YOU.
WATTO DOESN'T KNOW I'VE BUILT IT. YOU COULD MAKE HIM THINK IT WAS YOURS, AND YOU COULD GET HIM TO LET ME PILOT IT FOR YOU.
I DON'T WANT YOU TO RACE, ANNIE...
BUT, MOM, I LOVE IT...
...THE PRIZE MONEY WOULD MORE THAN PAY FOR THE PARTS THEY NEED.
YOUR MOTHER'S RIGHT. IS THERE ANYONE FRIENDLY TO THE REPUBLIC WHO CAN HELP US?
MOM... YOU SAID THAT THE BIGGEST PROBLEM IN THE UNIVERSE IS NO ONE HELPS EACH OTHER.
I'M SURE QUI-GON DOESN'T WANT TO PUT YOUR SON IN DANGER. WE WILL FIND SOME OTHER WAY.
NO, THERE IS NO OTHER WAY... I MAY NOT LIKE IT, BUT HE CAN HELP YOU...
HE WAS MEANT TO HELP YOU.

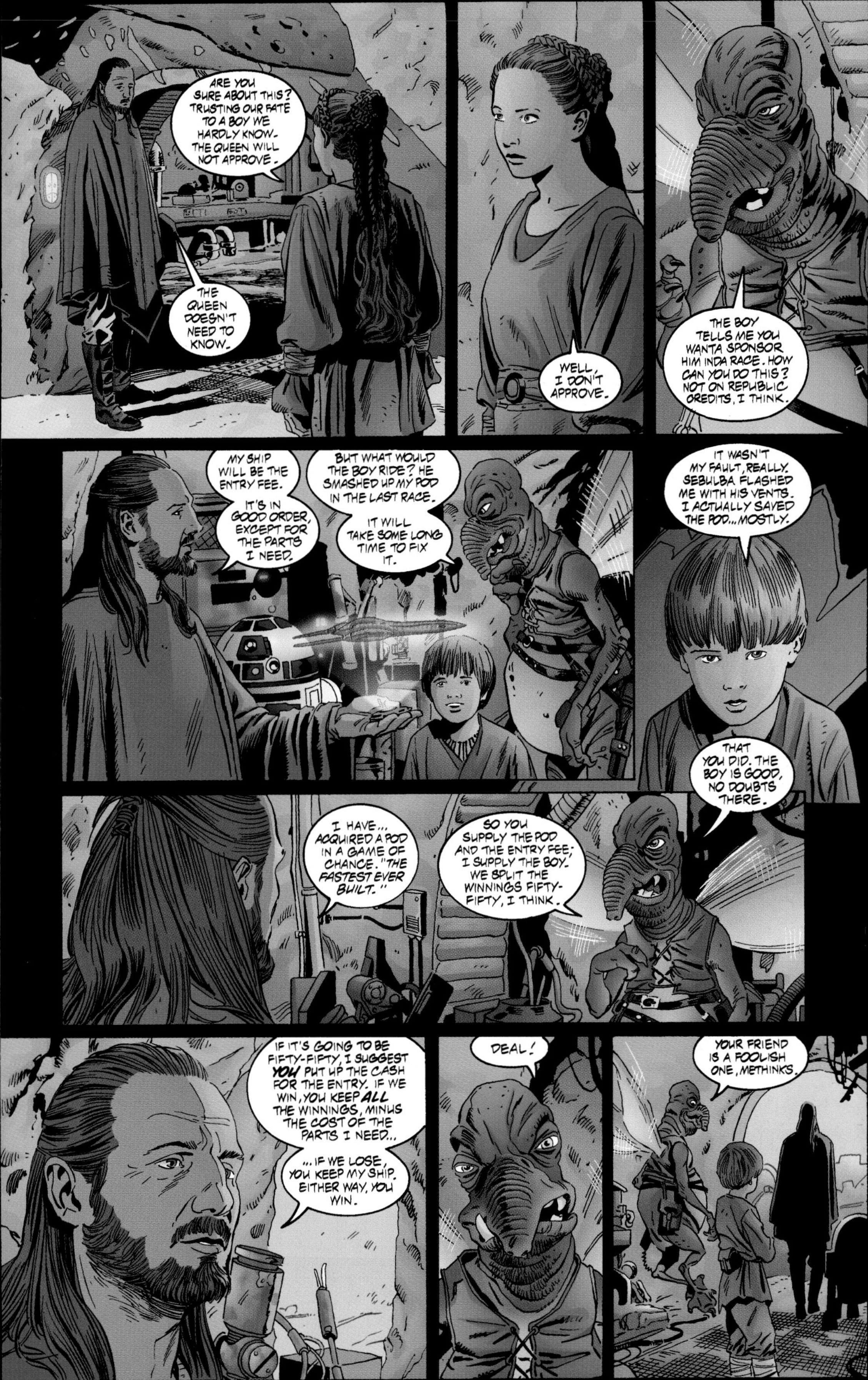

ARE YOU SURE ABOUT THIS? TRUSTING OUR FATE TO A BOY WE HARDLY KNOW. THE QUEEN WILL NOT APPROVE.
THE QUEEN DOESN'T NEED TO KNOW.
WELL, I DON'T APPROVE.
THE BOY TELLS ME YOU WANTA SPONSOR HIM INDA RACE. HOW CAN YOU DO THIS? NOT ON REPUBLIC CREDITS, I THINK.
MY SHIP WILL BE THE ENTRY FEE.
IT'S IN GOOD ORDER, EXCEPT FOR THE PARTS I NEED.
BUT WHAT WOULD THE BOY RIDE? HE SMASHED UP MY POD IN THE LAST RACE.
IT WILL TAKE SOME LONG TIME TO FIX IT.
IT WASN'T MY FAULT, REALLY. SEBULBA FLASHED ME WITH HIS VENTS. I ACTUALLY SAVED THE POD...MOSTLY.
THAT YOU DID. THE BOY IS GOOD, NO DOUBTS THERE.
I HAVE... ACQUIRED A POD IN A GAME OF CHANCE. "THE FASTEST EVER BUILT."
SO YOU SUPPLY THE POD AND THE ENTRY FEE; I SUPPLY THE BOY. WE SPLIT THE WINNINGS FIFTY-FIFTY, I THINK.
IF IT'S GOING TO BE FIFTY-FIFTY, I SUGGEST YOU PUT UP THE CASH FOR THE ENTRY. IF WE WIN, YOU KEEP ALL THE WINNINGS, MINUS THE COST OF THE PARTS I NEED...
...IF WE LOSE, YOU KEEP MY SHIP. EITHER WAY, YOU WIN.
DEAL!
YOUR FRIEND IS A FOOLISH ONE, METHINKS.

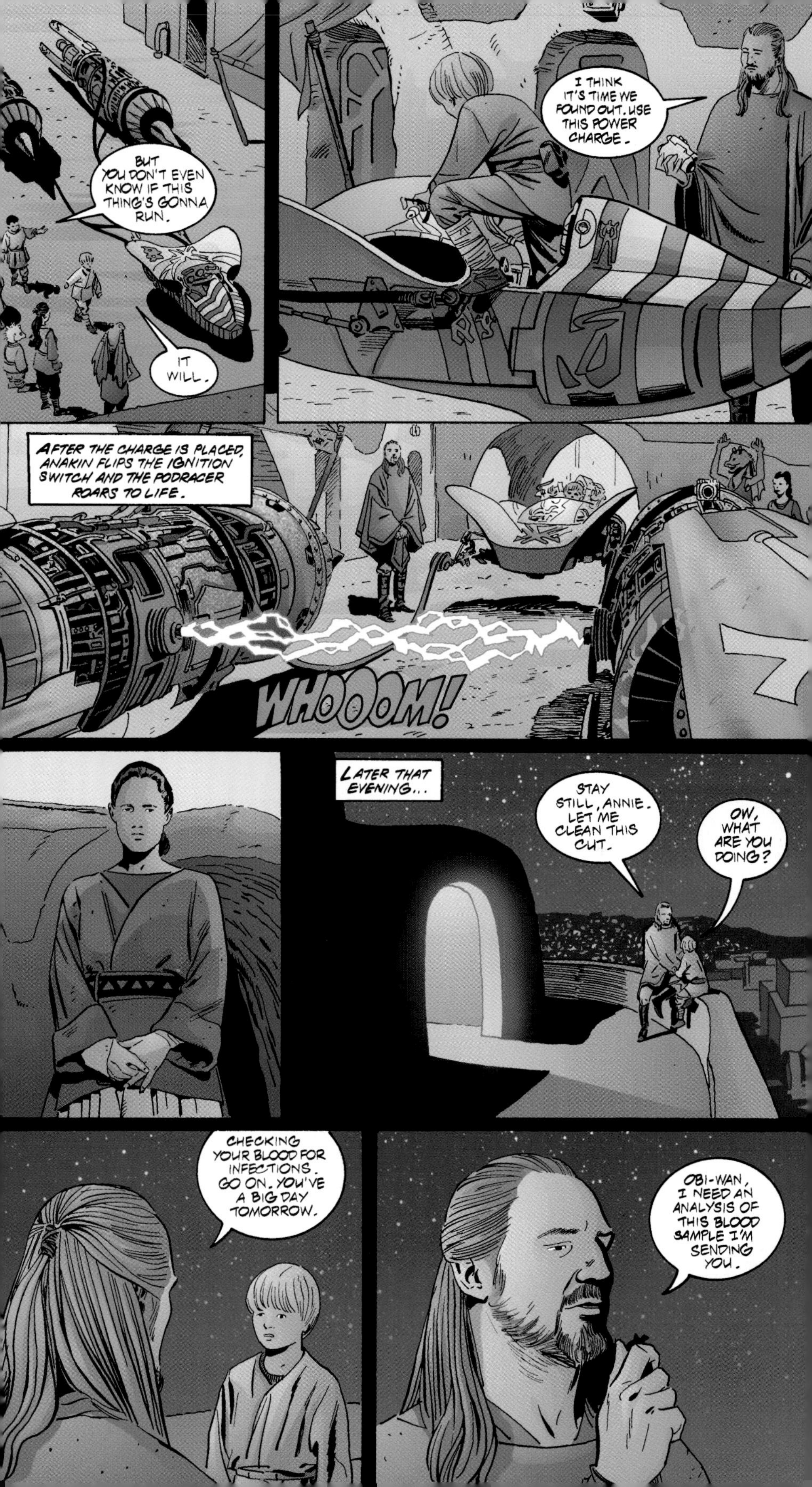
BUT YOU DON'T EVEN KNOW IF THIS THING'S GONNA RUN.
IT WILL.
I THINK IT'S TIME WE FOUND OUT. USE THIS POWER CHARGE.
AFTER THE CHARGE IS PLACED, ANAKIN FLIPS THE IGNITION SWITCH AND THE PODRACER ROARS TO LIFE.
WHOOOOM!
LATER THAT EVENING...
STAY STILL, ANNIE. LET ME CLEAN THIS CUT.
OW, WHAT ARE YOU DOING?
CHECKING YOUR BLOOD FOR INFECTIONS. GO ON. YOU'VE A BIG DAY TOMORROW.
OBI-WAN, I NEED AN ANALYSIS OF THIS BLOOD SAMPLE I'M SENDING YOU.

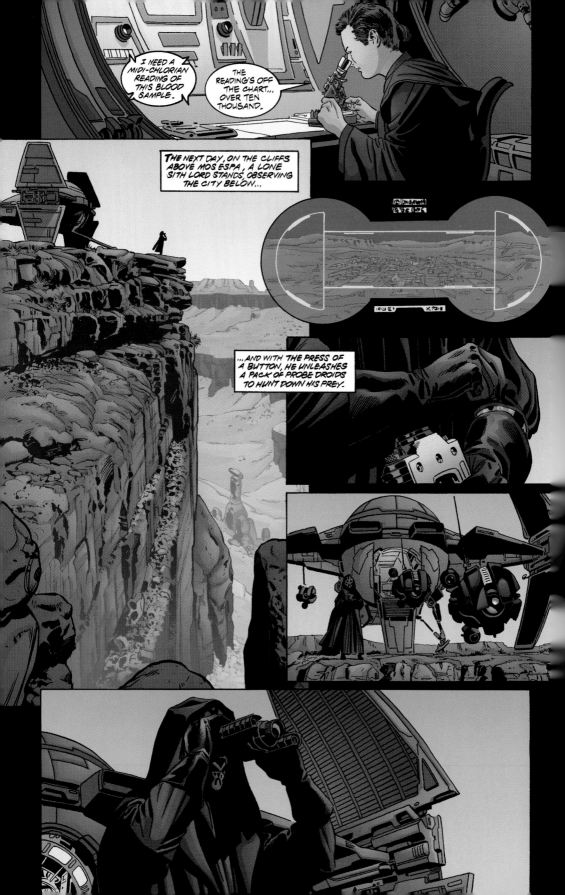

I NEED A MIDI-CHLORIAN READING OF THIS BLOOD SAMPLE.

THE READING'S OFF THE CHART... OVER TEN THOUSAND.

THE NEXT DAY, ON THE CLIFFS ABOVE MOS ESPA, A LONE SITH LORD STANDS, OBSERVING THE CITY BELOW...

...AND WITH *THE* PRESS OF A BUTTON, HE UNLEASHES A PACK OF PROBE DROIDS TO *HUNT* DOWN HIS PREY.

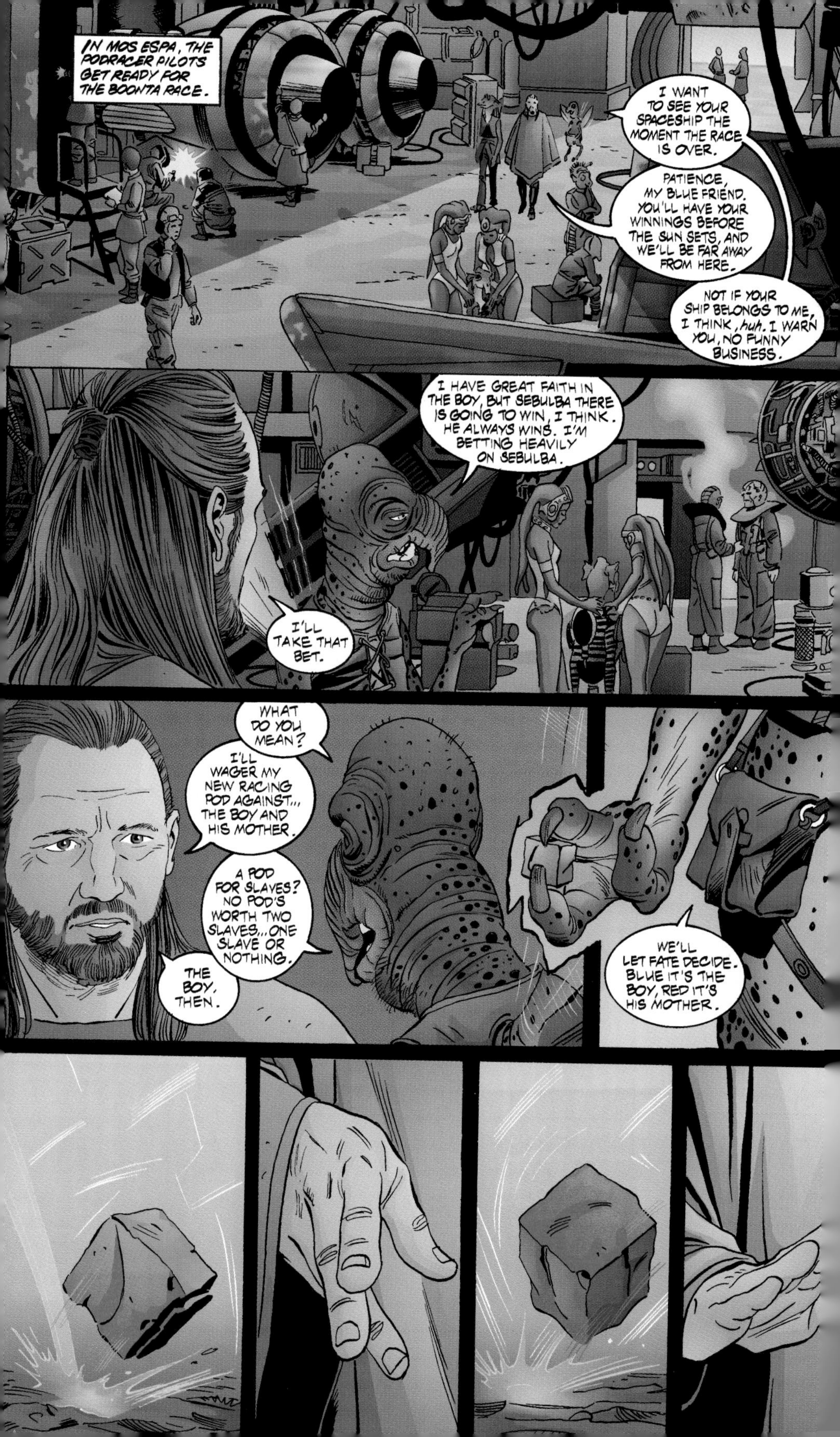
IN MOS ESPA, THE PODRACER PILOTS GET READY FOR THE BOONTA RACE.
I WANT TO SEE YOUR SPACESHIP THE MOMENT THE RACE IS OVER.
PATIENCE, MY BLUE FRIEND. YOU'LL HAVE YOUR WINNINGS BEFORE THE SUN SETS, AND WE'LL BE FAR AWAY FROM HERE.
NOT IF YOUR SHIP BELONGS TO ME, I THINK, huh. I WARN YOU, NO FUNNY BUSINESS.
I HAVE GREAT FAITH IN THE BOY, BUT SEBULBA THERE IS GOING TO WIN, I THINK. HE ALWAYS WINS. I'M BETTING HEAVILY ON SEBULBA.
I'LL TAKE THAT BET.
WHAT DO YOU MEAN?
I'LL WAGER MY NEW RACING POD AGAINST... THE BOY AND HIS MOTHER.
A POD FOR SLAVES? NO POD'S WORTH TWO SLAVES... ONE SLAVE OR NOTHING.
THE BOY, THEN.
WE'LL LET FATE DECIDE. BLUE IT'S THE BOY, RED IT'S HIS MOTHER.

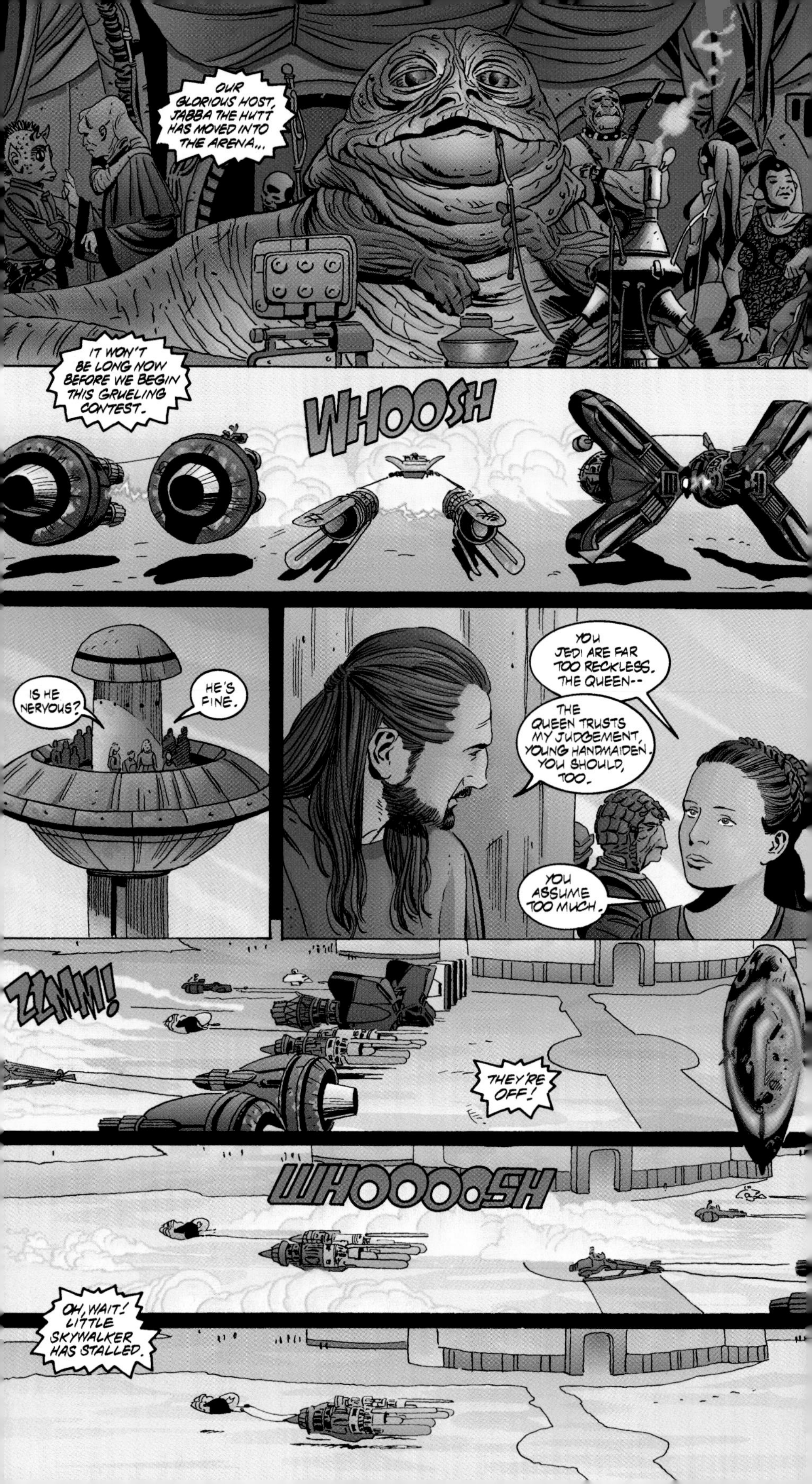
OUR GLORIOUS HOST, JABBA THE HUTT HAS MOVED INTO THE ARENA...
IT WON'T BE LONG NOW BEFORE WE BEGIN THIS GRUELING CONTEST.
WHOOSH
IS HE NERVOUS?
HE'S FINE.
YOU JEDI ARE FAR TOO RECKLESS. THE QUEEN--
THE QUEEN TRUSTS MY JUDGEMENT, YOUNG HANDMAIDEN. YOU SHOULD, TOO.
YOU ASSUME TOO MUCH.
ZZMMM!
THEY'RE OFF!
WHOOOOSH
OH, WAIT! LITTLE SKYWALKER HAS STALLED.

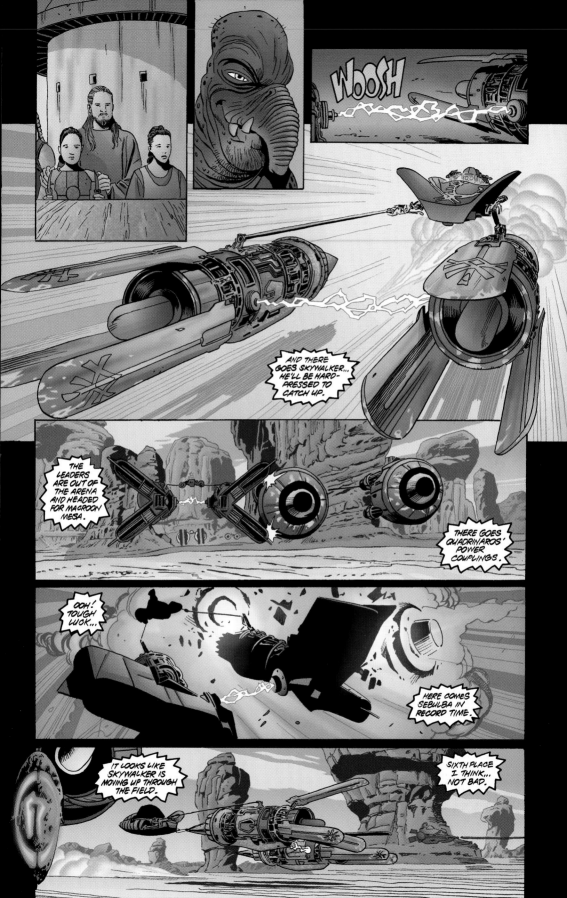

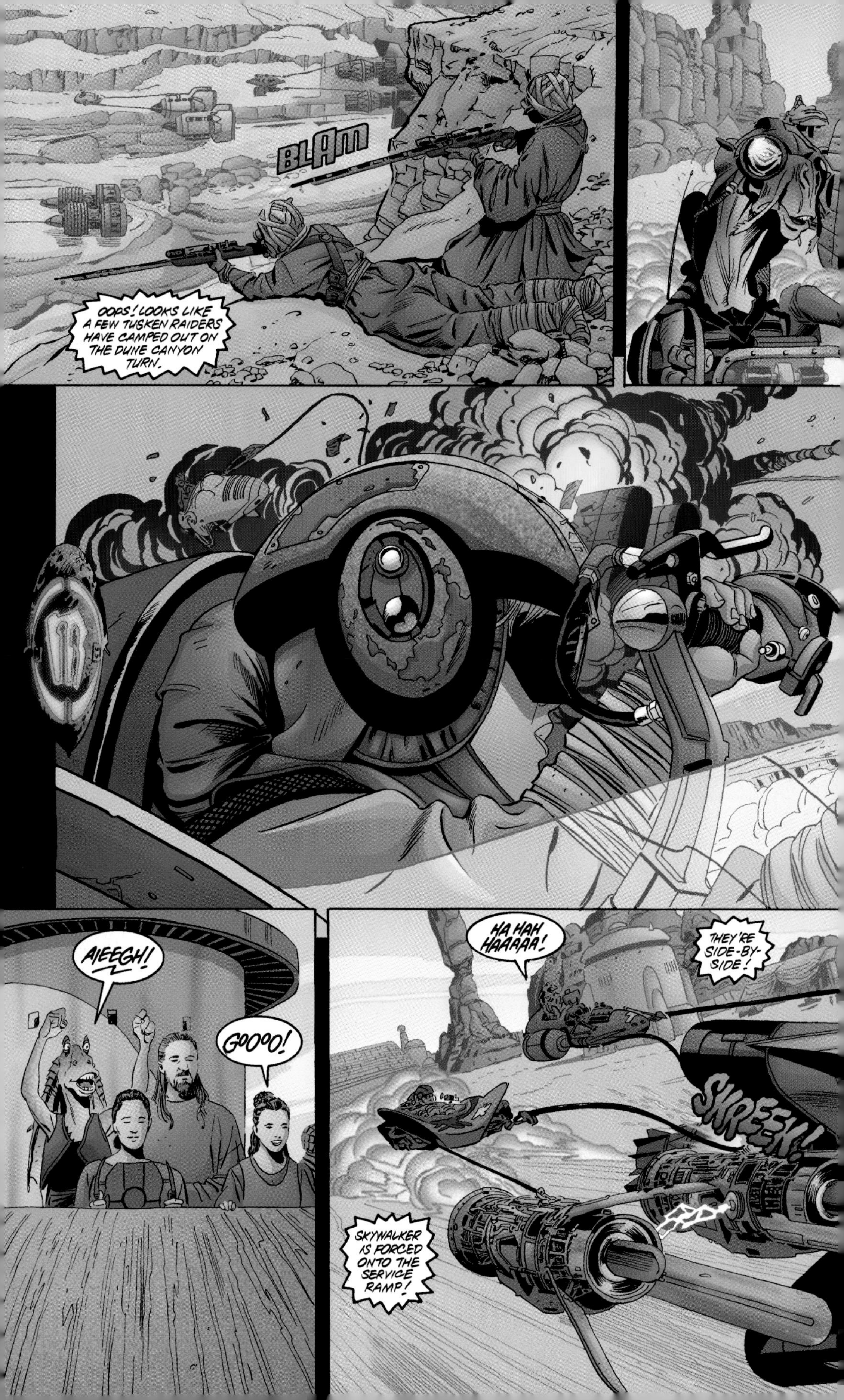
BLAM
OOPS! LOOKS LIKE A FEW TUSKEN RAIDERS HAVE CAMPED OUT ON THE DUNE CANYON TURN.
AIEEGH!
GOOOO!
HA HAH HAAAAA!
THEY'RE SIDE-BY-SIDE!
SKREEK!
SKYWALKER IS FORCED ONTO THE SERVICE RAMP!

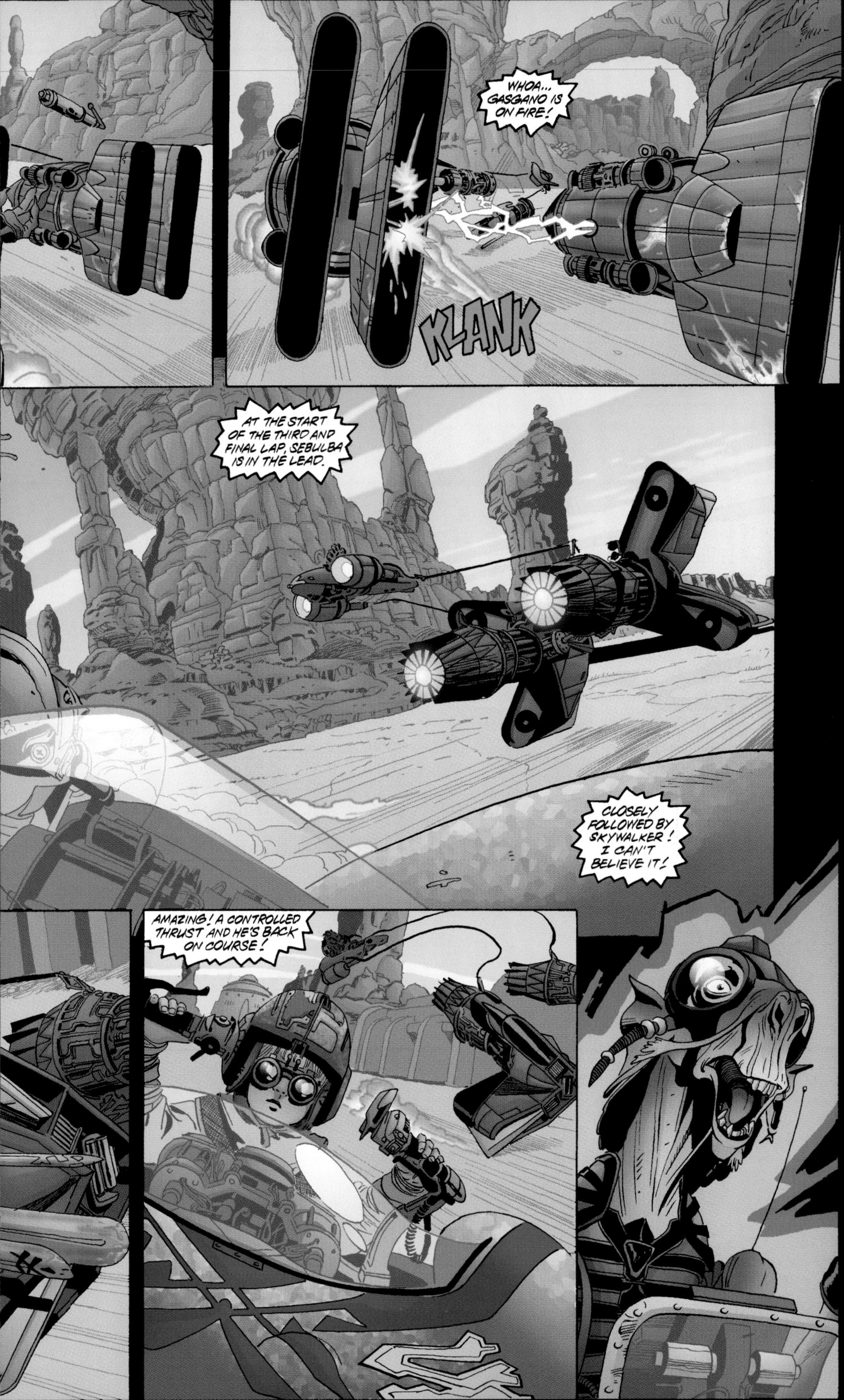
WHOA... GASGANO IS ON FIRE!
KLANK
AT THE START OF THE THIRD AND FINAL LAP, SEBULBA IS IN THE LEAD.
CLOSELY FOLLOWED BY SKYWALKER! I CAN'T BELIEVE IT!
AMAZING! A CONTROLLED THRUST AND HE'S BACK ON COURSE!

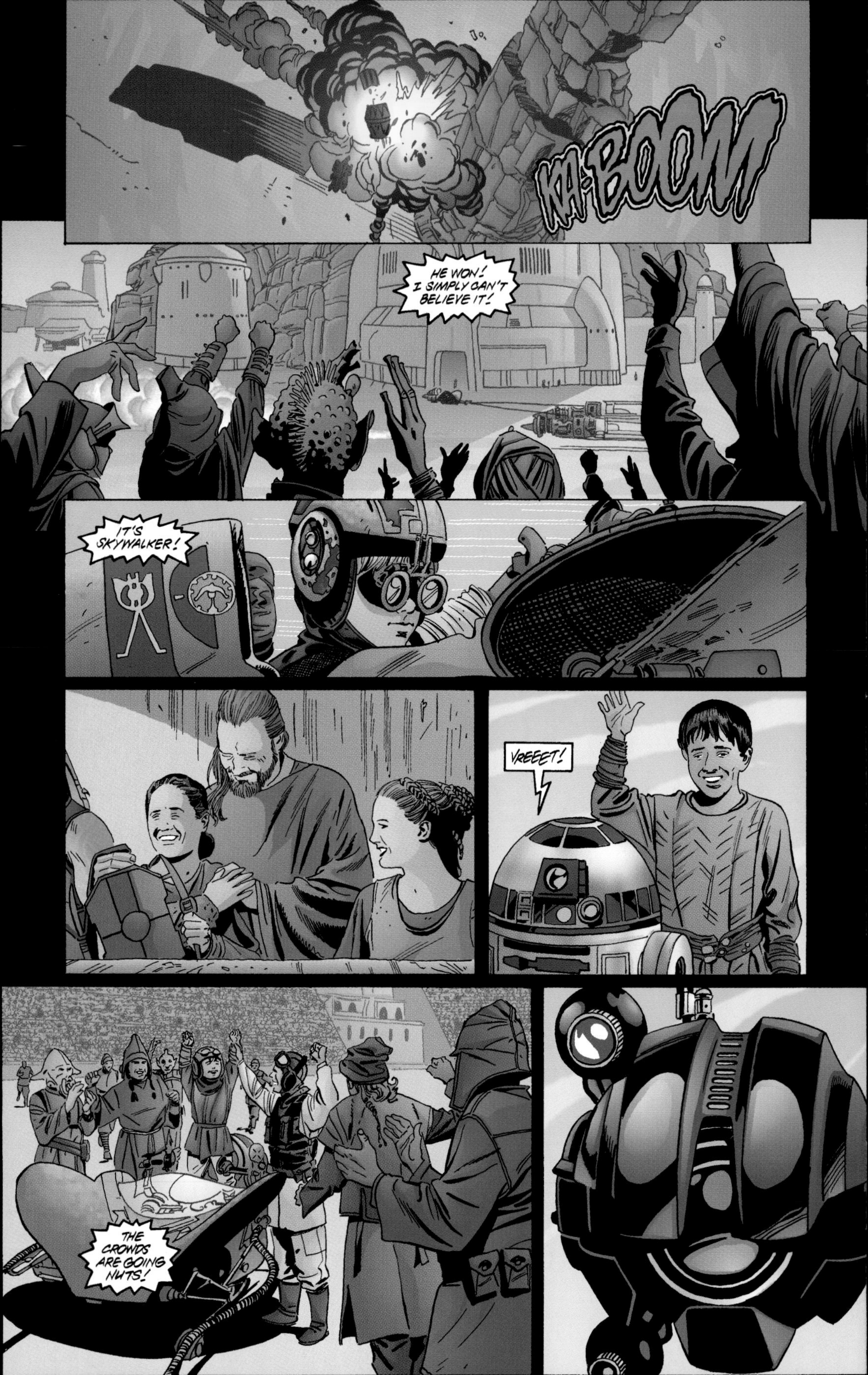
KA-BOOM
HE WON! I SIMPLY CAN'T BELIEVE IT!
IT'S SKYWALKER!
VREEET!
THE CROWDS ARE GOING NUTS!

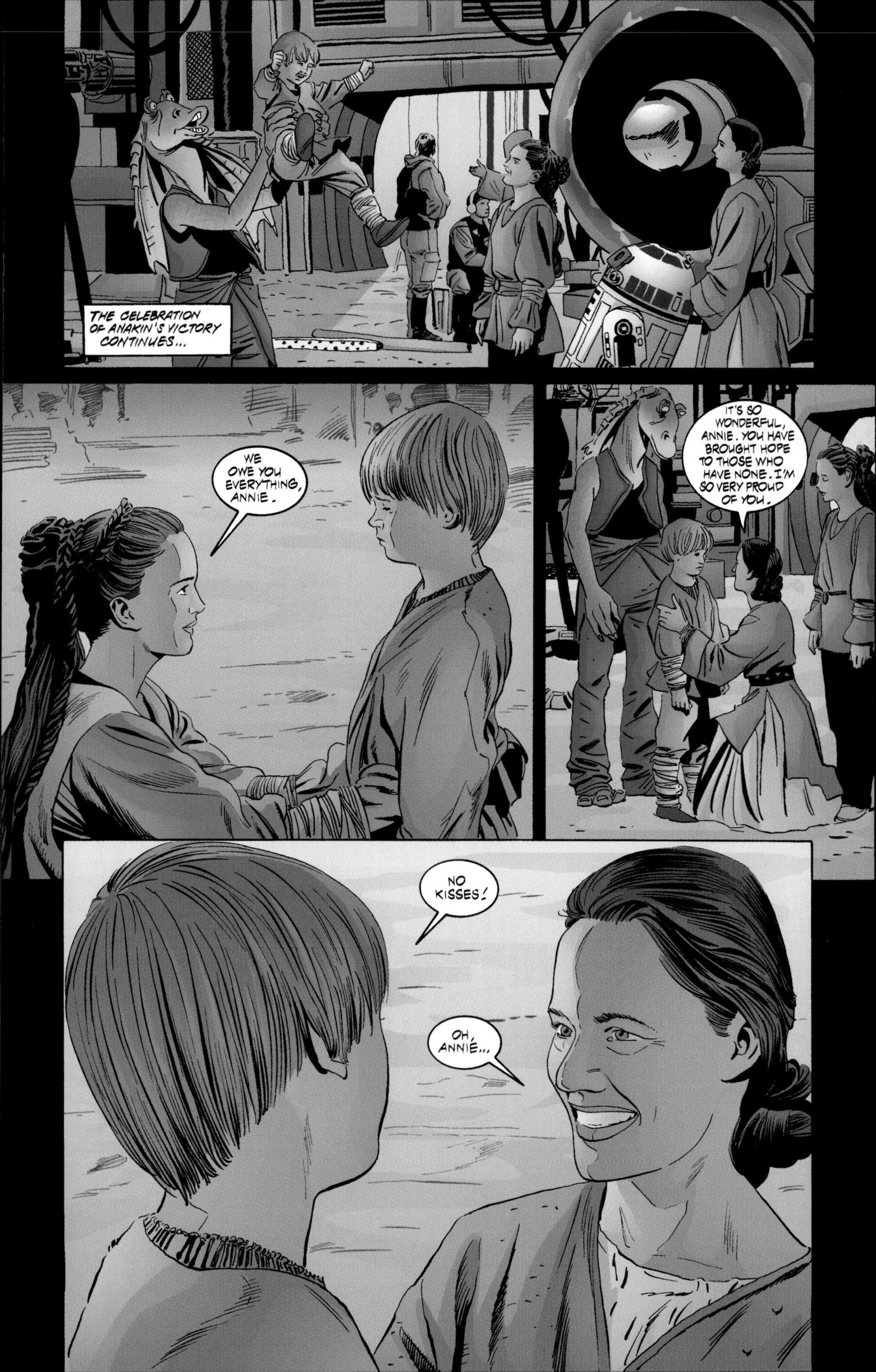
THE CELEBRATION OF ANAKIN'S VICTORY CONTINUES...
WE OWE YOU EVERYTHING, ANNIE.
IT'S SO WONDERFUL, ANNIE. YOU HAVE BROUGHT HOPE TO THOSE WHO HAVE NONE. I'M SO VERY PROUD OF YOU.
NO KISSES!
OH, ANNIE...

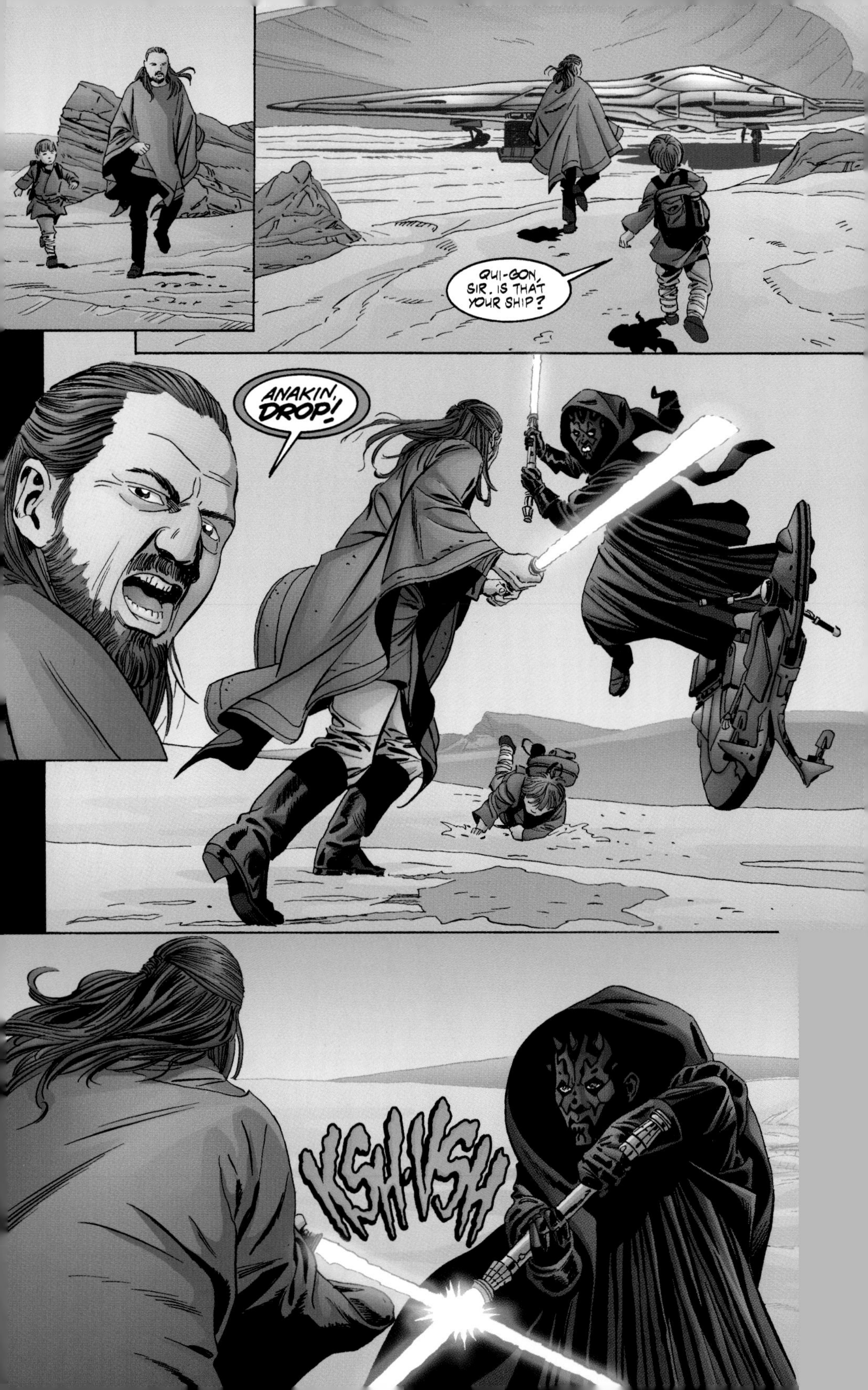
QUI-GON, SIR. IS THAT YOUR SHIP?
ANAKIN, DROP!
VSH-VSH

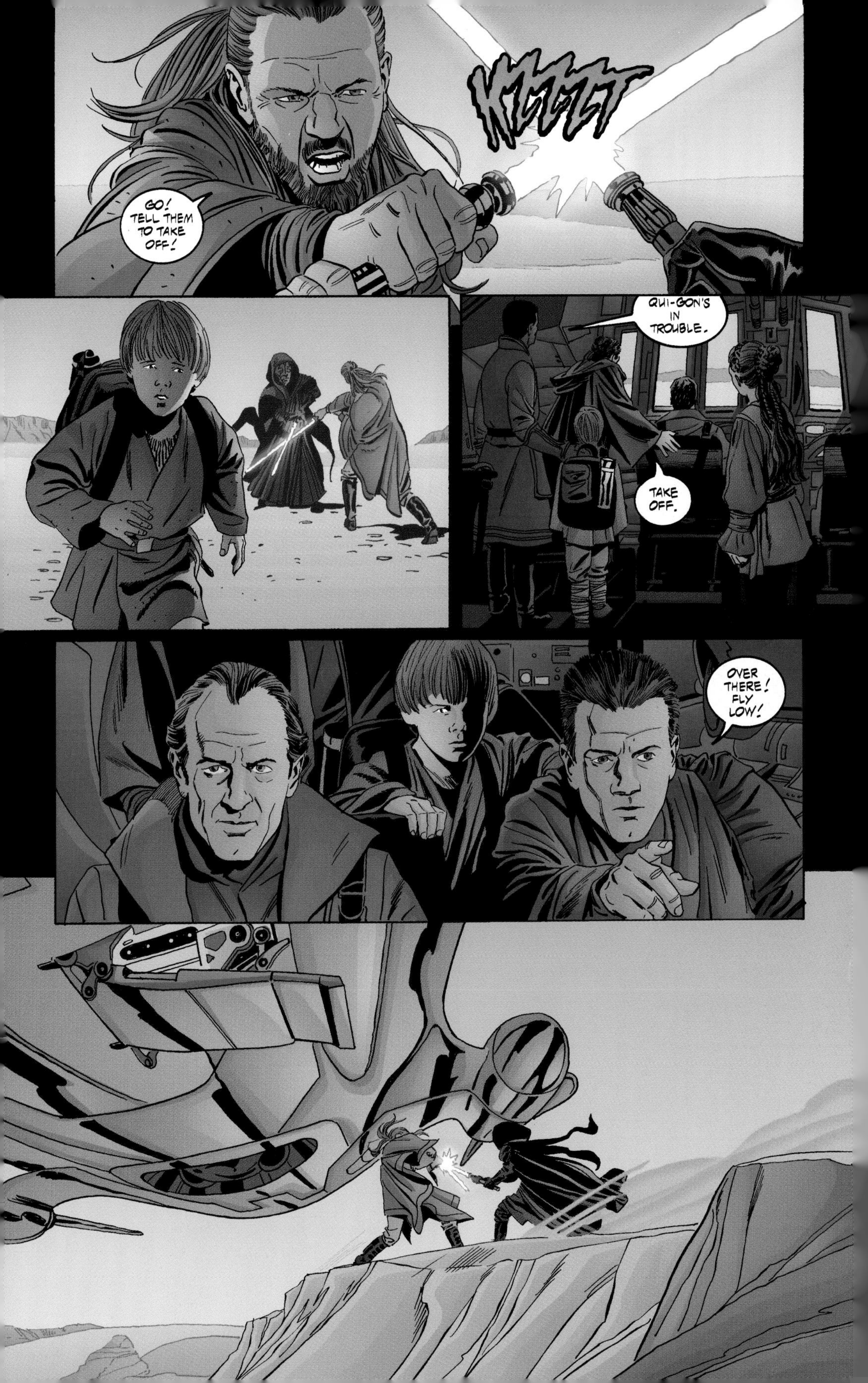
KZZZT
GO! TELL THEM TO TAKE OFF!
QUI-GON'S IN TROUBLE.
TAKE OFF.
OVER THERE! FLY LOW!

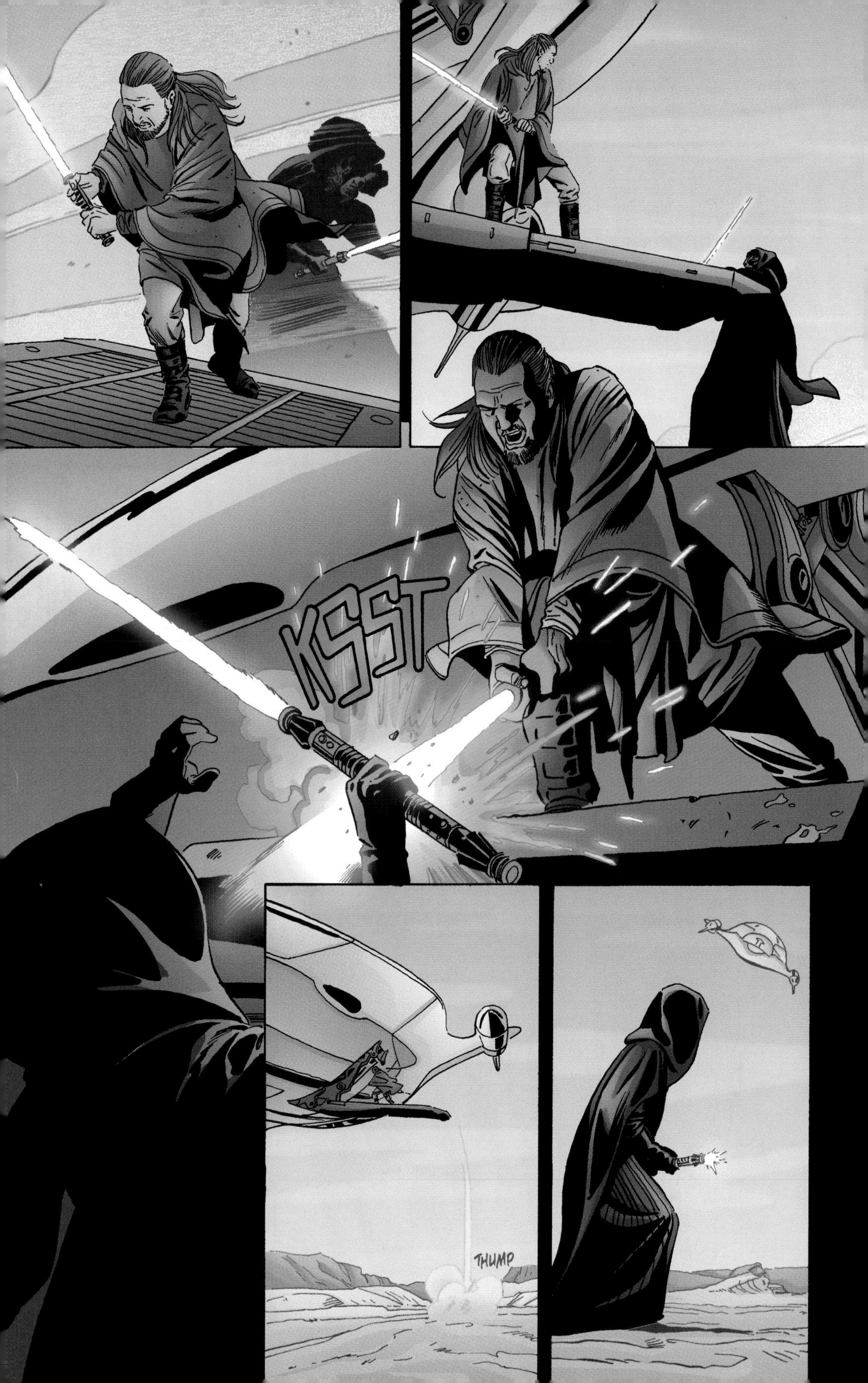
KSST
THUMP

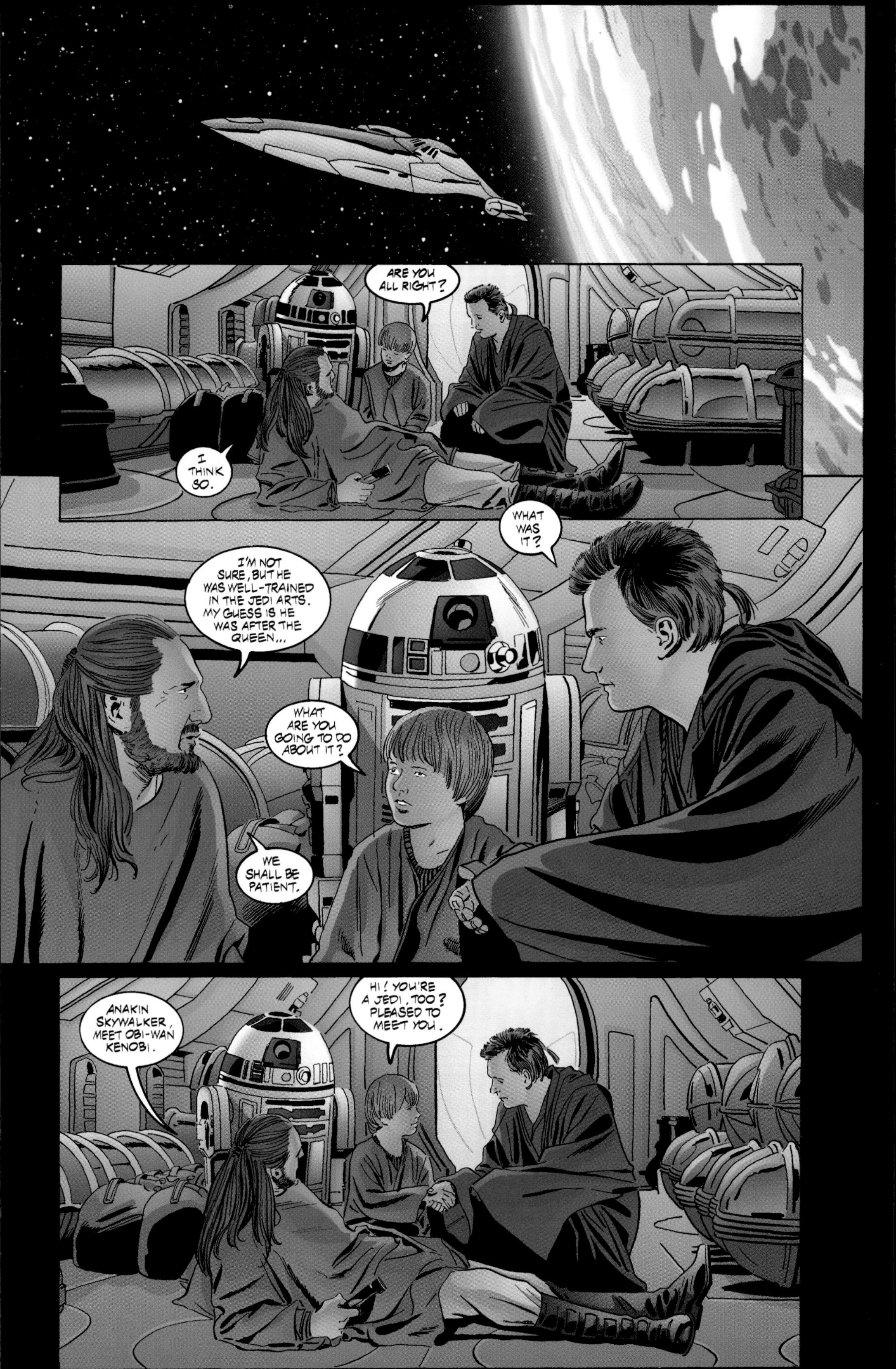
ARE YOU ALL RIGHT?
I THINK SO.
WHAT WAS IT?
I'M NOT SURE, BUT HE WAS WELL-TRAINED IN THE JEDI ARTS. MY GUESS IS HE WAS AFTER THE QUEEN...
WHAT ARE YOU GOING TO DO ABOUT IT?
WE SHALL BE PATIENT.
ANAKIN SKYWALKER, MEET OBI-WAN KENOBI.
HI! YOU'RE A JEDI, TOO? PLEASED TO MEET YOU.

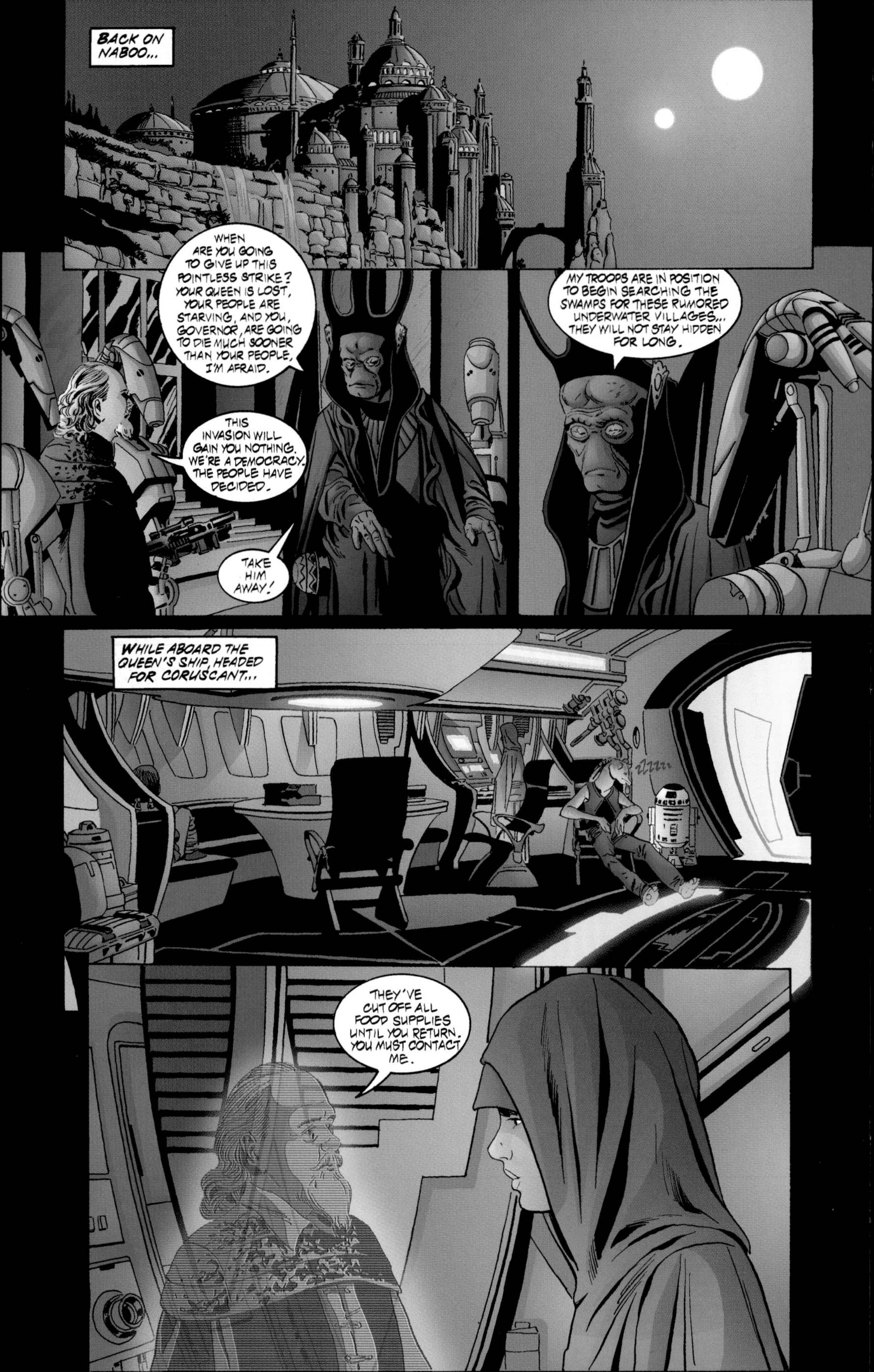
BACK ON NABOO...
WHEN ARE YOU GOING TO GIVE UP THIS POINTLESS STRIKE? YOUR QUEEN IS LOST, YOUR PEOPLE ARE STARVING, AND YOU, GOVERNOR, ARE GOING TO DIE MUCH SOONER THAN YOUR PEOPLE, I'M AFRAID.
THIS INVASION WILL GAIN YOU NOTHING. WE'RE A DEMOCRACY. THE PEOPLE HAVE DECIDED.
TAKE HIM AWAY!
MY TROOPS ARE IN POSITION TO BEGIN SEARCHING THE SWAMPS FOR THESE RUMORED UNDERWATER VILLAGES... THEY WILL NOT STAY HIDDEN FOR LONG.
WHILE ABOARD THE QUEEN'S SHIP, HEADED FOR CORUSCANT...
ZZZZZ...
THEY'VE CUT OFF ALL FOOD SUPPLIES UNTIL YOU RETURN. YOU MUST CONTACT ME.

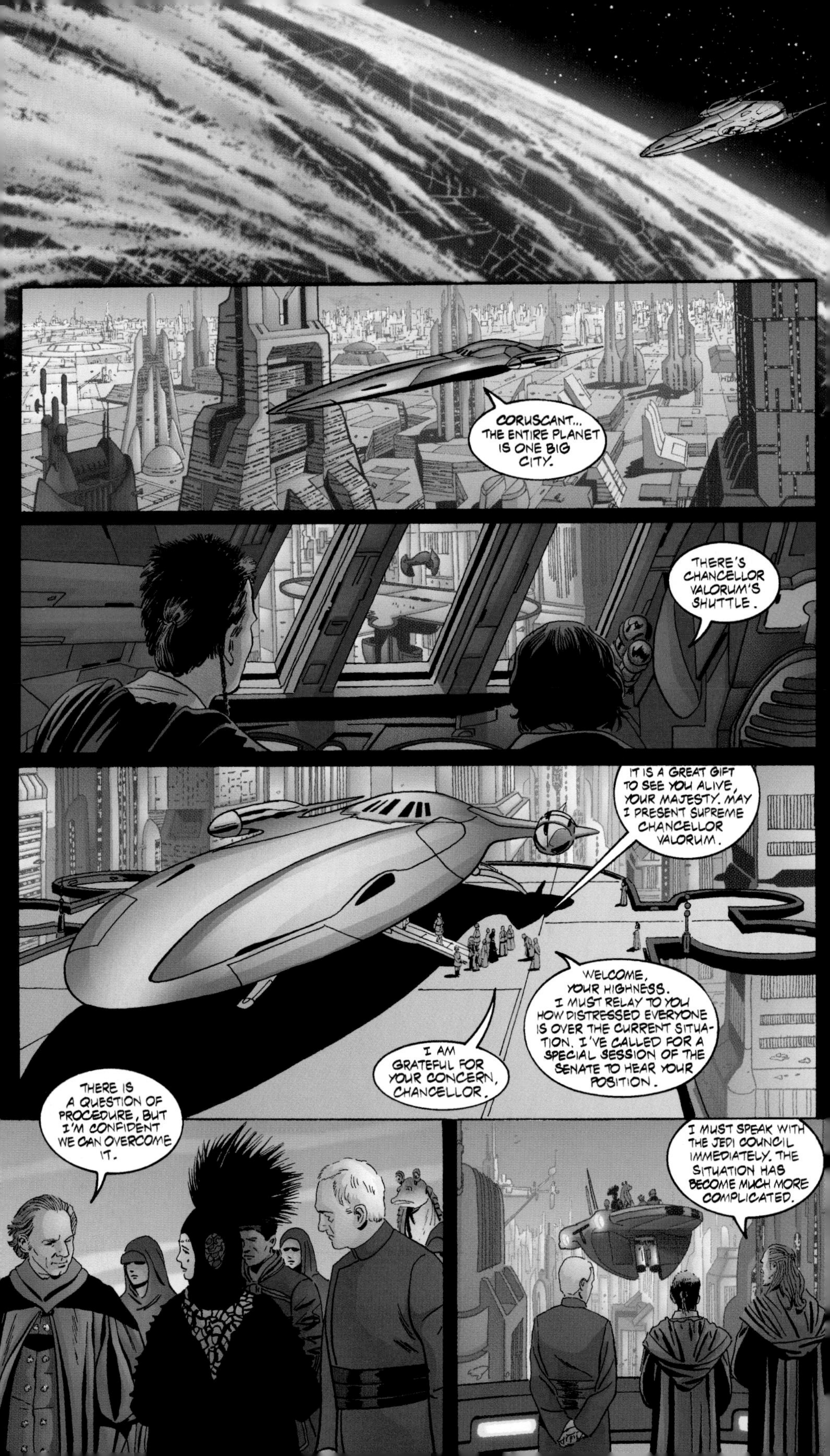
CORUSCANT... THE ENTIRE PLANET IS ONE BIG CITY.
THERE'S CHANCELLOR VALORUM'S SHUTTLE.
IT IS A GREAT GIFT TO SEE YOU ALIVE, YOUR MAJESTY. MAY I PRESENT SUPREME CHANCELLOR VALORUM.
WELCOME, YOUR HIGHNESS. I MUST RELAY TO YOU HOW DISTRESSED EVERYONE IS OVER THE CURRENT SITUATION. I'VE CALLED FOR A SPECIAL SESSION OF THE SENATE TO HEAR YOUR POSITION.
I AM GRATEFUL FOR YOUR CONCERN, CHANCELLOR.
THERE IS A QUESTION OF PROCEDURE, BUT I'M CONFIDENT WE CAN OVERCOME IT.
I MUST SPEAK WITH THE JEDI COUNCIL IMMEDIATELY. THE SITUATION HAS BECOME MUCH MORE COMPLICATED.

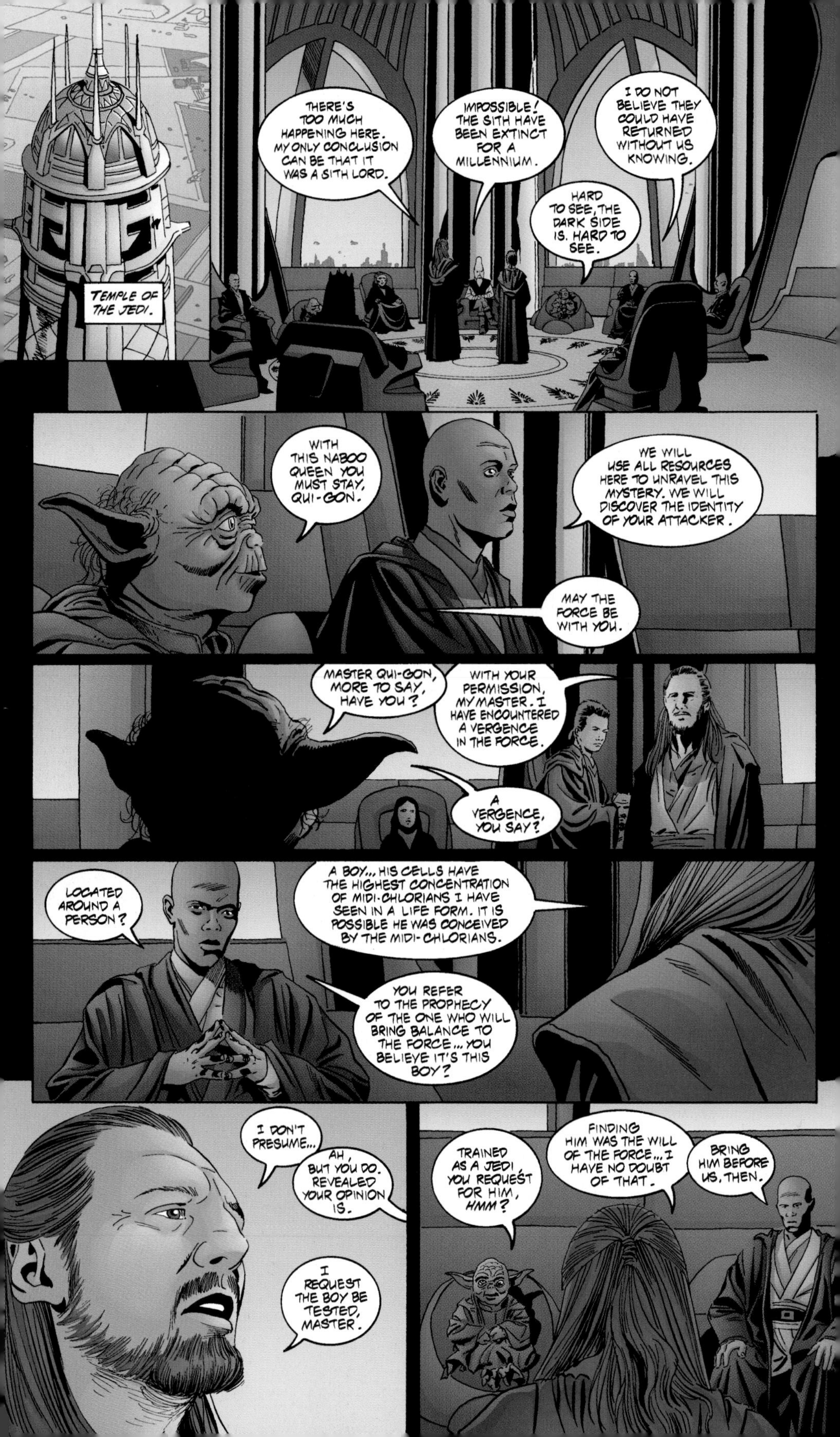
TEMPLE OF THE JEDI.
THERE'S TOO MUCH HAPPENING HERE. MY ONLY CONCLUSION CAN BE THAT IT WAS A SITH LORD.
IMPOSSIBLE! THE SITH HAVE BEEN EXTINCT FOR A MILLENNIUM.
I DO NOT BELIEVE THEY COULD HAVE RETURNED WITHOUT US KNOWING.
HARD TO SEE, THE DARK SIDE IS. HARD TO SEE.
WITH THIS NABOO QUEEN YOU MUST STAY, QUI-GON.
WE WILL USE ALL RESOURCES HERE TO UNRAVEL THIS MYSTERY. WE WILL DISCOVER THE IDENTITY OF YOUR ATTACKER.
MAY THE FORCE BE WITH YOU.
MASTER QUI-GON, MORE TO SAY, HAVE YOU?
WITH YOUR PERMISSION, MY MASTER. I HAVE ENCOUNTERED A VERGENCE IN THE FORCE.
A VERGENCE, YOU SAY?
LOCATED AROUND A PERSON?
A BOY... HIS CELLS HAVE THE HIGHEST CONCENTRATION OF MIDI-CHLORIANS I HAVE SEEN IN A LIFE FORM. IT IS POSSIBLE HE WAS CONCEIVED BY THE MIDI-CHLORIANS.
YOU REFER TO THE PROPHECY OF THE ONE WHO WILL BRING BALANCE TO THE FORCE... YOU BELIEVE IT'S THIS BOY?
I DON'T PRESUME...
AH, BUT YOU DO. REVEALED YOUR OPINION IS.
I REQUEST THE BOY BE TESTED, MASTER.
TRAINED AS A JEDI, YOU REQUEST FOR HIM, HMM?
FINDING HIM WAS THE WILL OF THE FORCE... I HAVE NO DOUBT OF THAT.
BRING HIM BEFORE US, THEN.

THERE IS NO PROOF. THIS IS INCREDIBLE. WE RECOMMEND A COMMISSION BE SENT TO NABOO TO ASCERTAIN THE TRUTH.

THE CONGRESS OF MALASTARE CONCURS WITH THE HONORABLE DELEGATION FROM THE TRADE FEDERATION. A COMMISSION MUST BE APPOINTED.

YOUR HONOR, YOU CANNOT ALLOW US TO BE CONDEMNED WITHOUT REASONABLE OBSERVATION.

IT'S ALL RULES OF PROCEDURE.

ENTER THE BUREAUCRATS, THE TRUE RULERS OF THE REPUBLIC, AND ON THE PAYROLL OF THE TRADE FEDERATION, I MIGHT ADD. THIS IS WHERE CHANCELLOR VALORUM'S STRENGTH WILL DISAPPEAR.

THE POINT IS CONCEDED. WILL YOU DEFER YOUR MOTION TO ALLOW A COMMISSION TO EXPLORE THE VALIDITY OF YOUR ACCUSA- TIONS?

I WILL NOT DEFER...

I HAVE COME BEFORE YOU TO RESOLVE THIS ATTACK ON OUR SOVEREIGNTY NOW. I WAS NOT ELECTED TO WATCH MY PEOPLE SUFFER AND DIE WHILE YOU DISCUSS THIS INVASION IN A COMMITTEE.

THE TRADE FEDERATION MOVES THE MOTION BE SENT TO THE PROCEDURES COMMITTEE FOR STUDY.

IF THIS BODY IS NOT CAPABLE OF ACTION, I SUGGEST NEW LEADERSHIP IS NEEDED.

I MOVE FOR A "VOTE OF NO CONFIDENCE" IN CHANCELLOR VALORUM'S LEADER- SHIP.

NEW LEADERSHIP! A VOTE!

NEW LEADERSHIP! A VOTE!

A VOTE!

ORDER! WE SHALL HAVE ORDER!

NEW LEADERSHIP! A VOTE!

THEY WILL ELECT IN A NEW CHANCEL- LOR, A STRONG CHANCELLOR, ONE WHO WILL NOT LET OUR TRAGEDY CONTINUE.

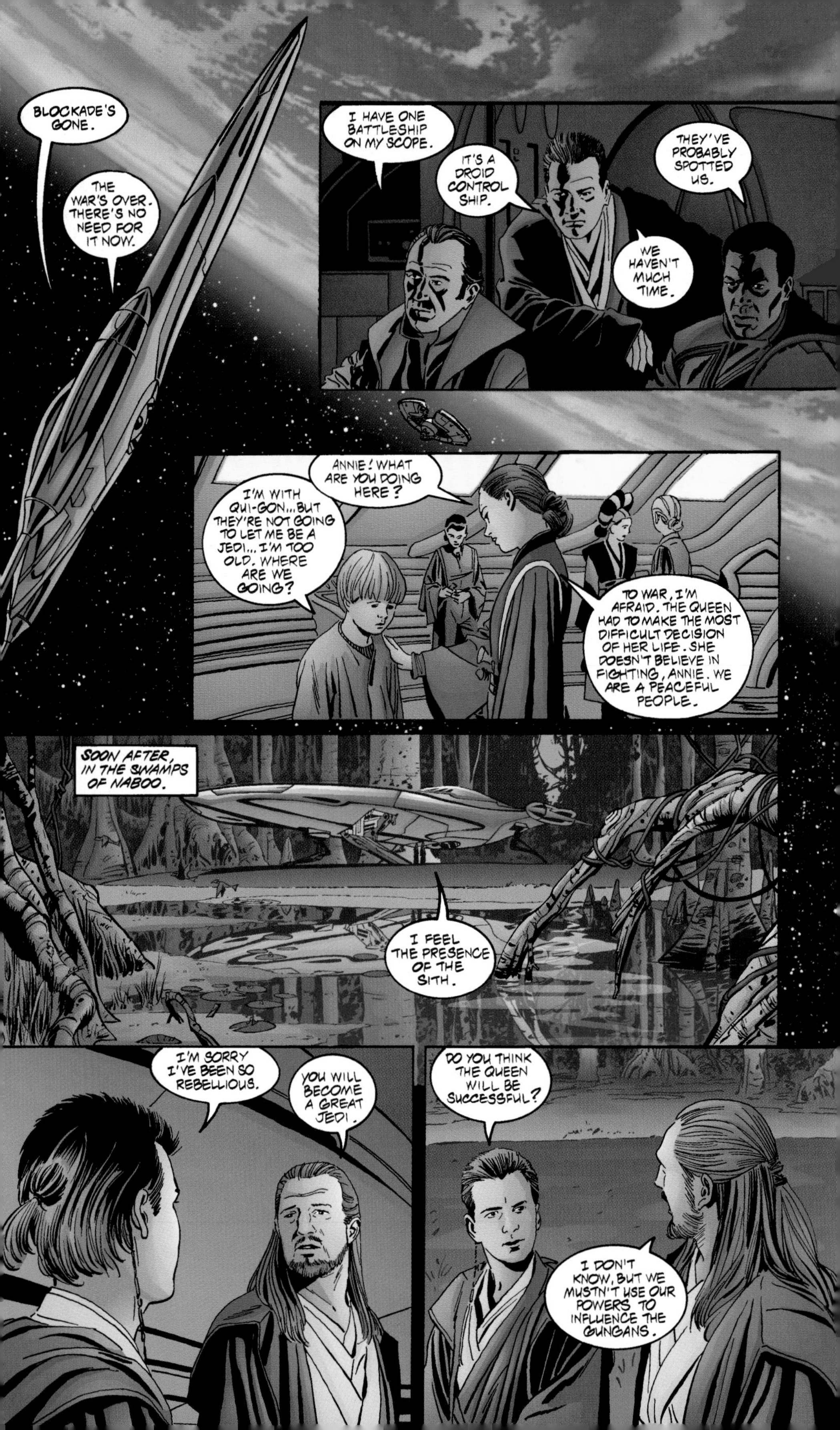
BLOCKADE'S GONE.
THE WAR'S OVER. THERE'S NO NEED FOR IT NOW.
I HAVE ONE BATTLESHIP ON MY SCOPE.
IT'S A DROID CONTROL SHIP.
THEY'VE PROBABLY SPOTTED US.
WE HAVEN'T MUCH TIME.
ANNIE! WHAT ARE YOU DOING HERE?
I'M WITH QUI-GON... BUT THEY'RE NOT GOING TO LET ME BE A JEDI... I'M TOO OLD. WHERE ARE WE GOING?
TO WAR, I'M AFRAID. THE QUEEN HAD TO MAKE THE MOST DIFFICULT DECISION OF HER LIFE. SHE DOESN'T BELIEVE IN FIGHTING, ANNIE. WE ARE A PEACEFUL PEOPLE.
SOON AFTER, IN THE SWAMPS OF NABOO.
I FEEL THE PRESENCE OF THE SITH.
I'M SORRY I'VE BEEN SO REBELLIOUS.
YOU WILL BECOME A GREAT JEDI.
DO YOU THINK THE QUEEN WILL BE SUCCESSFUL?
I DON'T KNOW, BUT WE MUSTN'T USE OUR POWERS TO INFLUENCE THE GUNGANS.

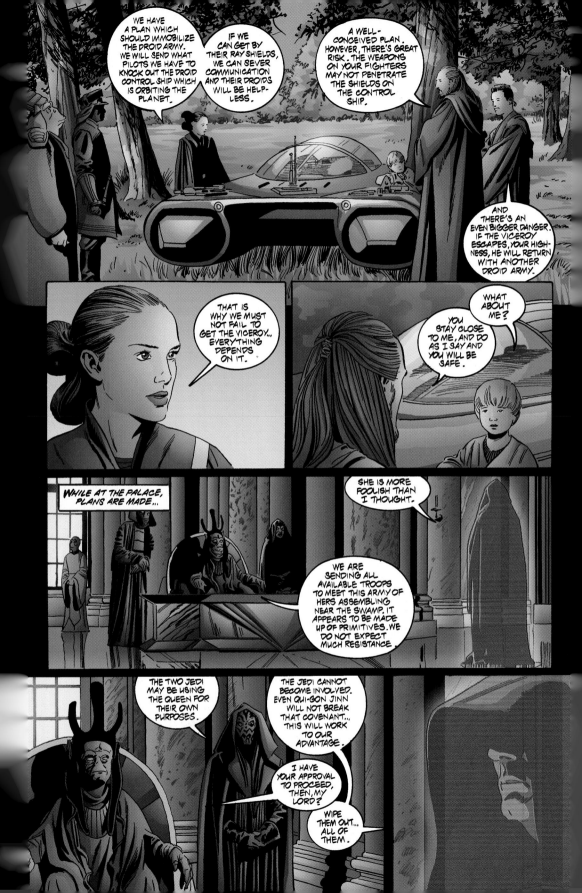

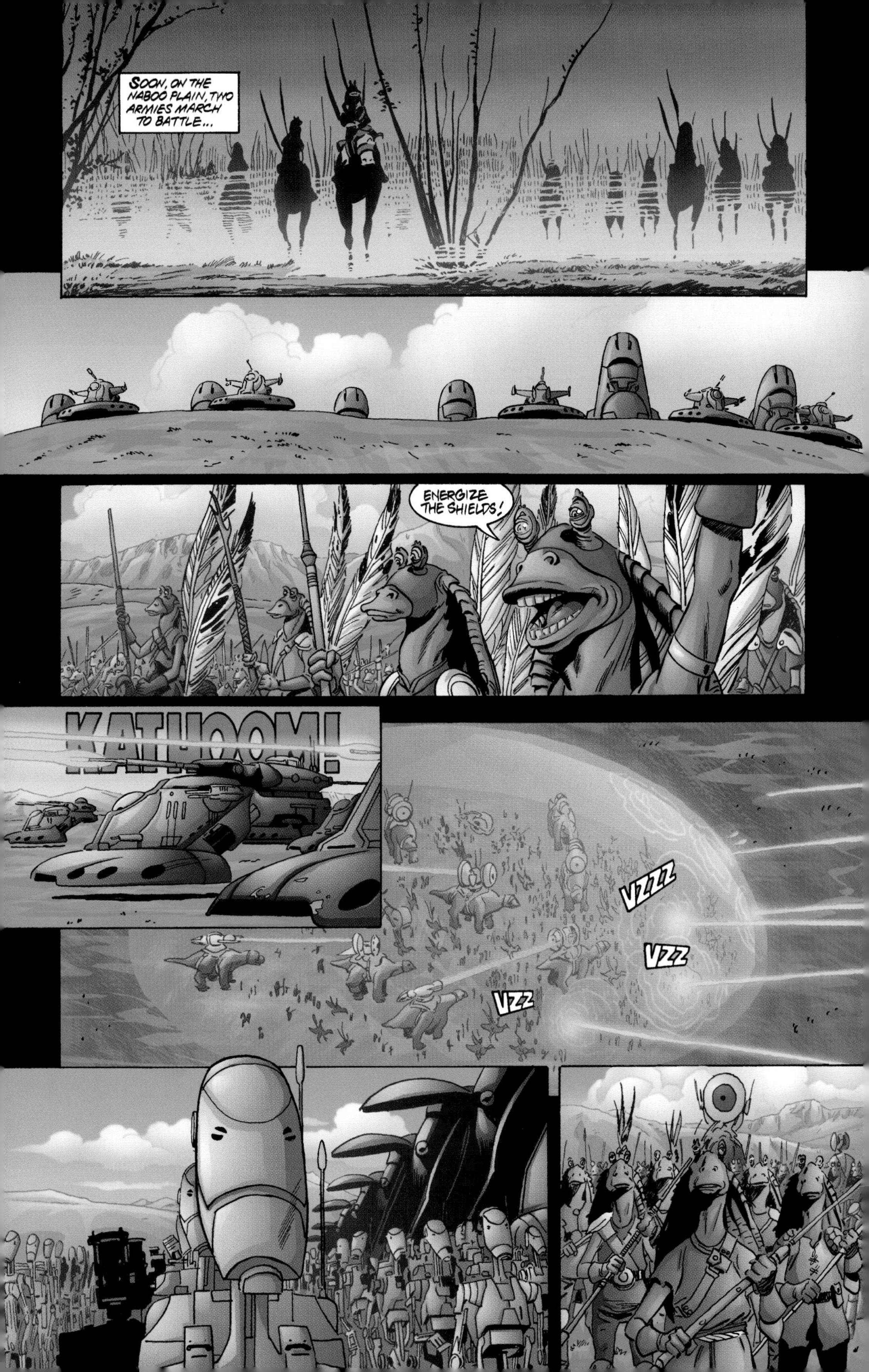
SOON, ON THE NABOO PLAIN, TWO ARMIES MARCH TO BATTLE...
ENERGIZE THE SHIELDS!
KATHOOM!
VZZZZ
VZZ
VZZ

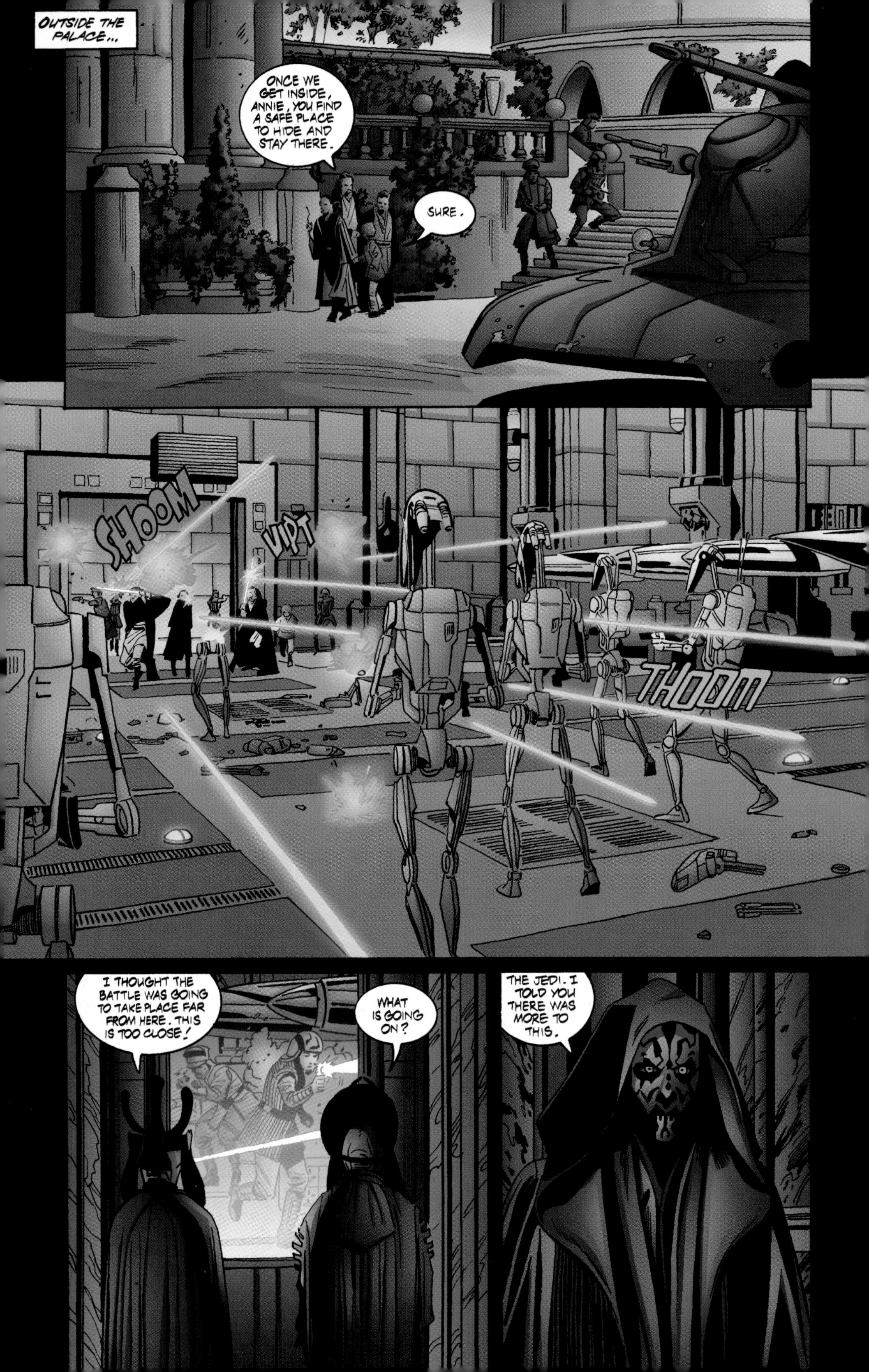
OUTSIDE THE PALACE...
ONCE WE GET INSIDE, ANNIE, YOU FIND A SAFE PLACE TO HIDE AND STAY THERE.
SURE.
SHOOM
VIPT
THOOM
I THOUGHT THE BATTLE WAS GOING TO TAKE PLACE FAR FROM HERE. THIS IS TOO CLOSE!
WHAT IS GOING ON?
THE JEDI. I TOLD YOU THERE WAS MORE TO THIS.

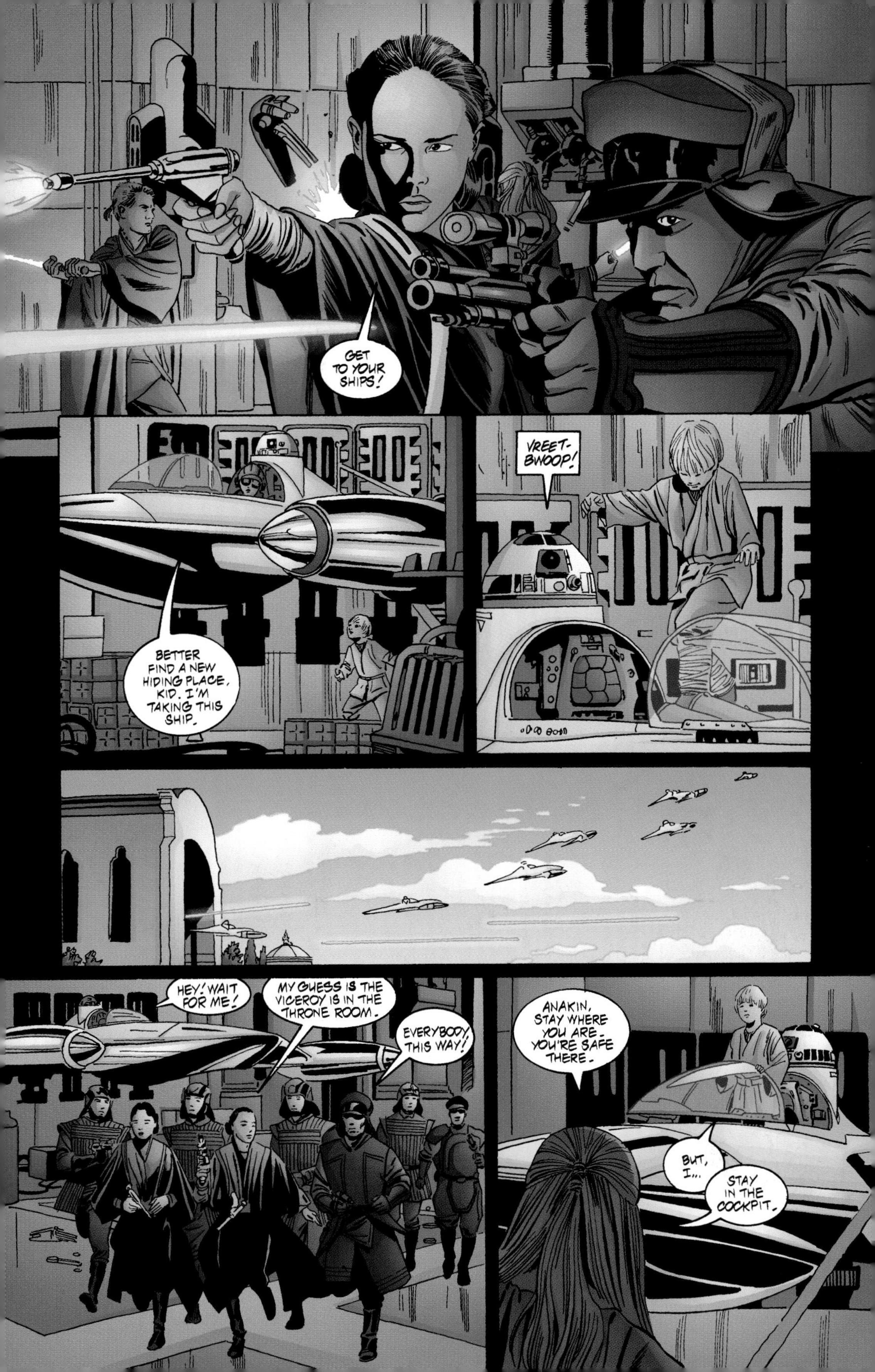
GET TO YOUR SHIPS!
BETTER FIND A NEW HIDING PLACE, KID. I'M TAKING THIS SHIP.
VREET-BWOOP!
HEY! WAIT FOR ME!
MY GUESS IS THE VICEROY IS IN THE THRONE ROOM.
EVERYBODY, THIS WAY!
ANAKIN, STAY WHERE YOU ARE. YOU'RE SAFE THERE.
BUT, I...
STAY IN THE COCKPIT.

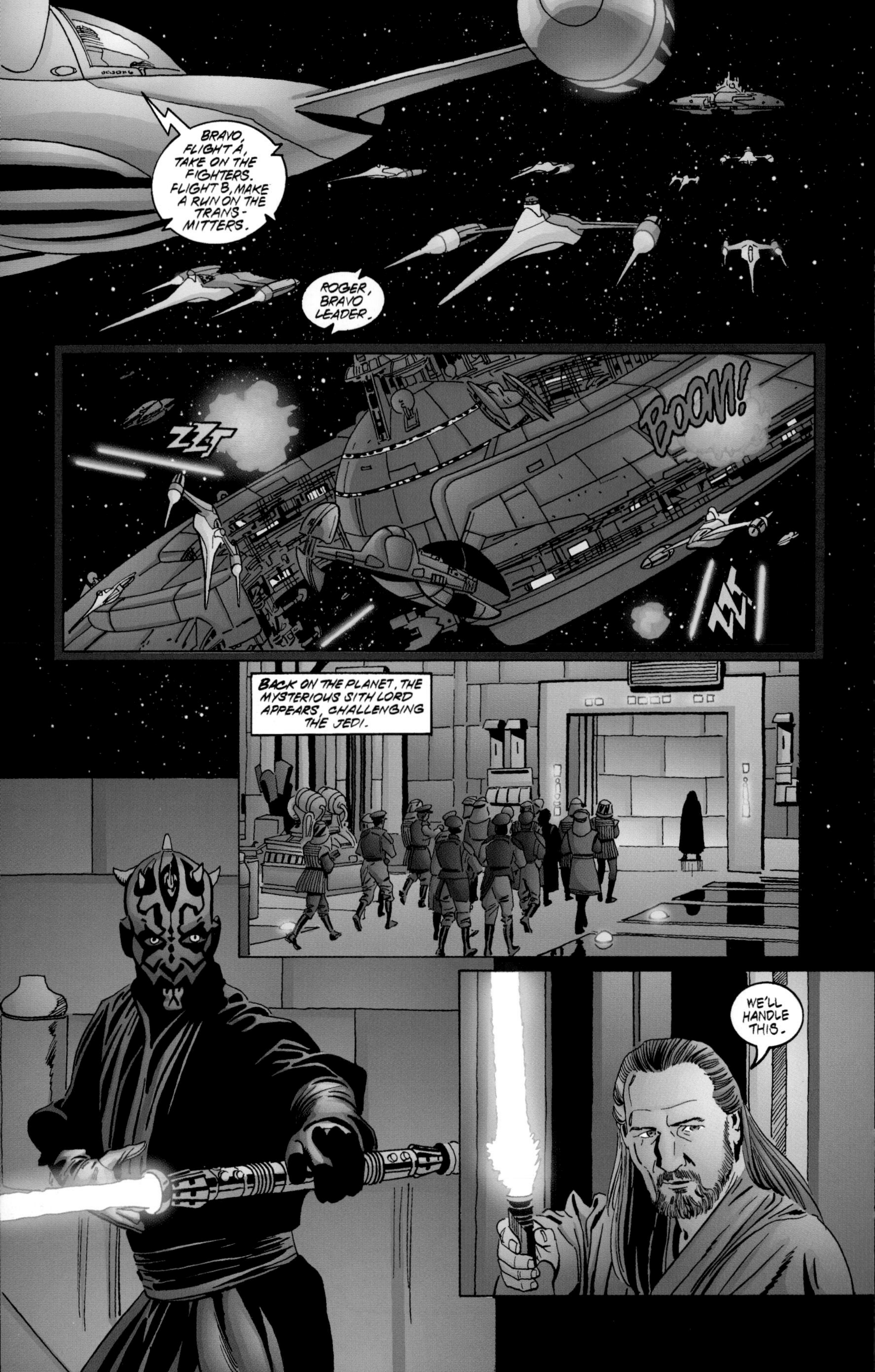
BRAVO, FLIGHT A, TAKE ON THE FIGHTERS. FLIGHT B, MAKE A RUN ON THE TRANS-MITTERS.
ROGER, BRAVO LEADER.
ZZT
BOOM!
ZZT
BACK ON THE PLANET, THE MYSTERIOUS SITH LORD APPEARS, CHALLENGING THE JEDI.
WE'LL HANDLE THIS.

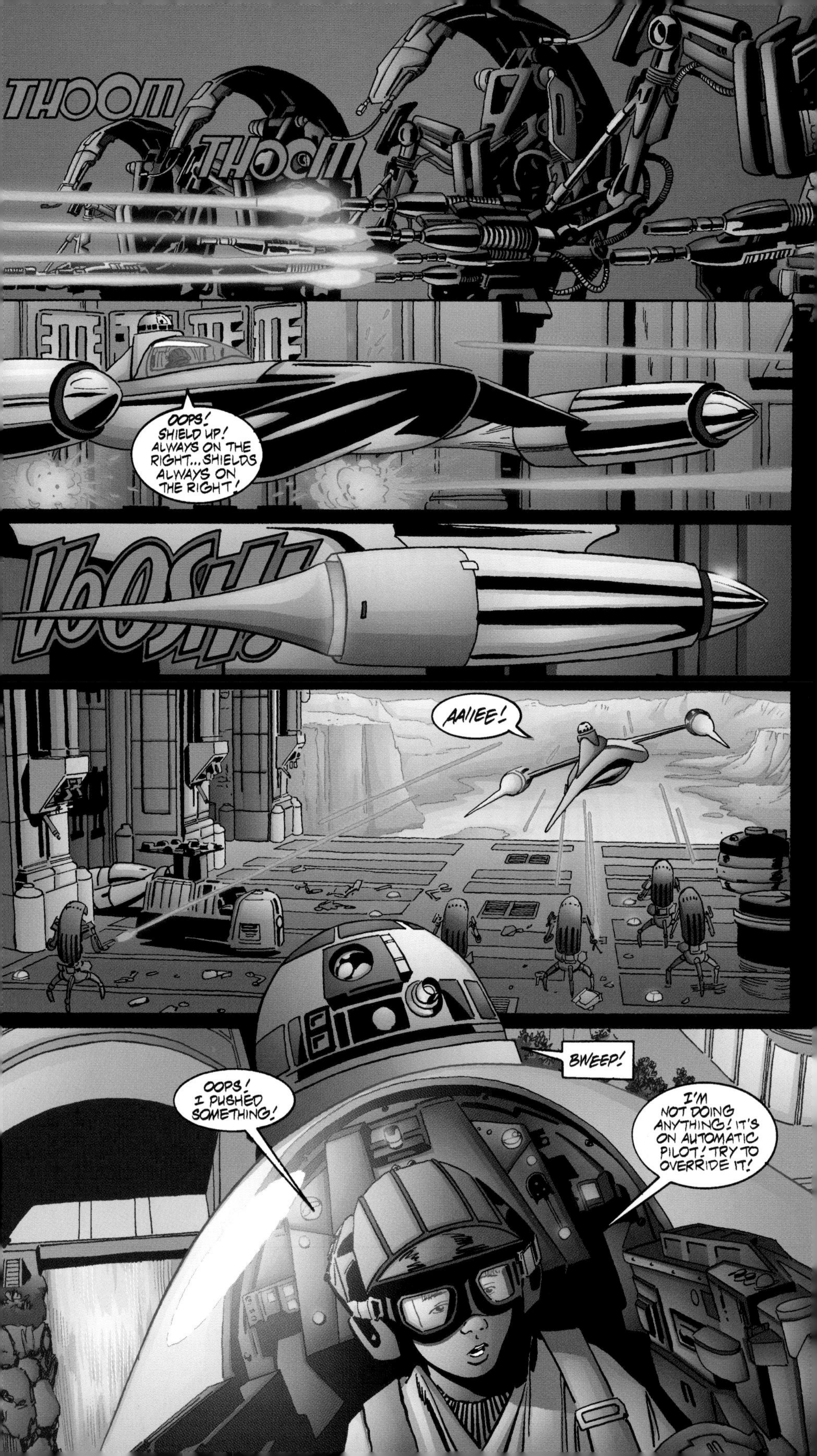
THOOM
THOOM
OOPS! SHIELD UP! ALWAYS ON THE RIGHT... SHIELDS ALWAYS ON THE RIGHT!
AAIIEE!
BWEEP!
OOPS! I PUSHED SOMETHING!
I'M NOT DOING ANYTHING! IT'S ON AUTOMATIC PILOT! TRY TO OVERRIDE IT!

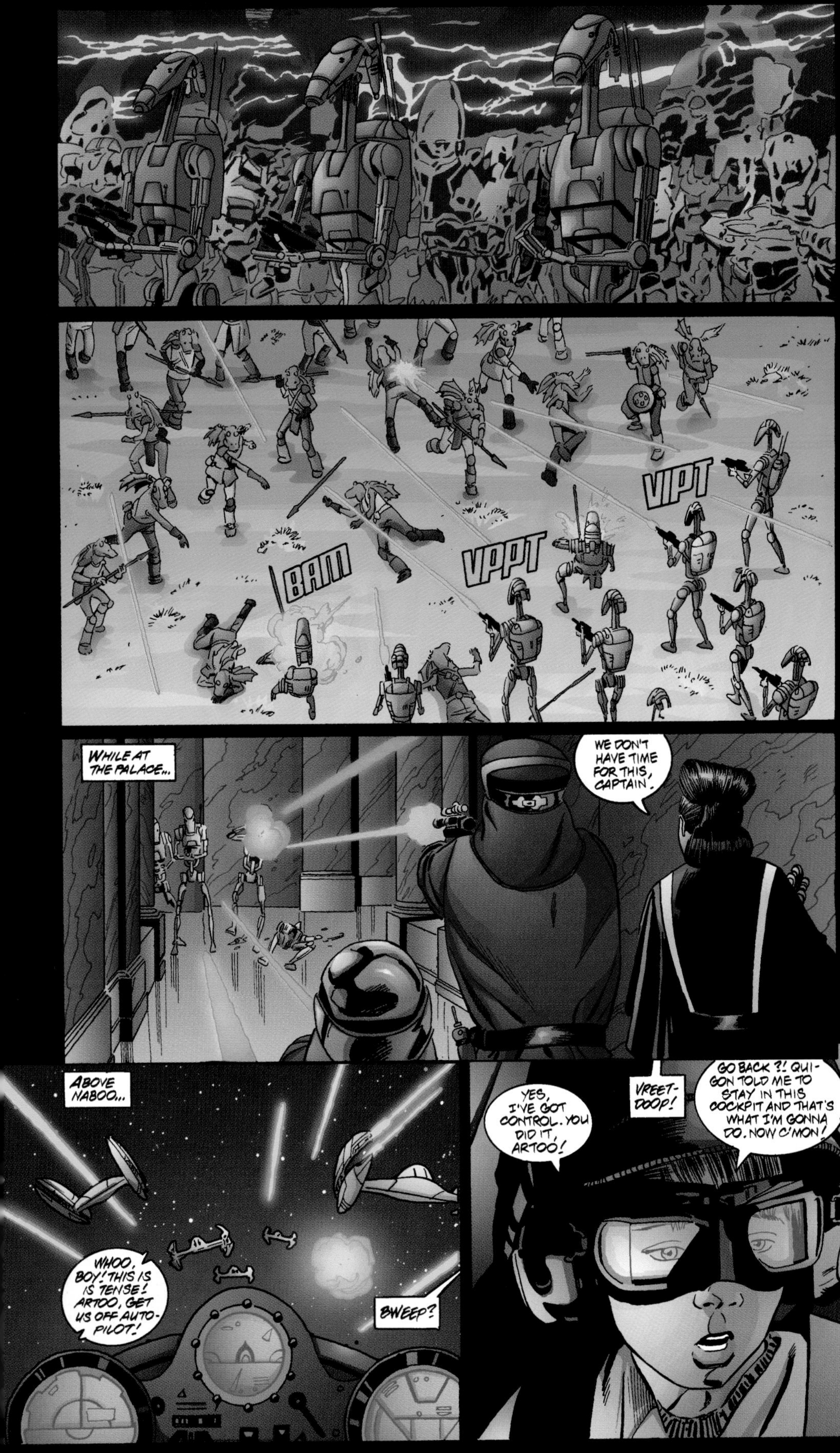
BAM
VPPT
VIPT
WHILE AT THE PALACE...
WE DON'T HAVE TIME FOR THIS, CAPTAIN.
ABOVE NABOO...
WHOO, BOY! THIS IS TENSE! ARTOO, GET US OFF AUTO-PILOT!
BWEEP?
YES, I'VE GOT CONTROL. YOU DID IT, ARTOO!
VREET-DOOP!
GO BACK ?! QUI-GON TOLD ME TO STAY IN THIS COCKPIT AND THAT'S WHAT I'M GONNA DO. NOW C'MON!

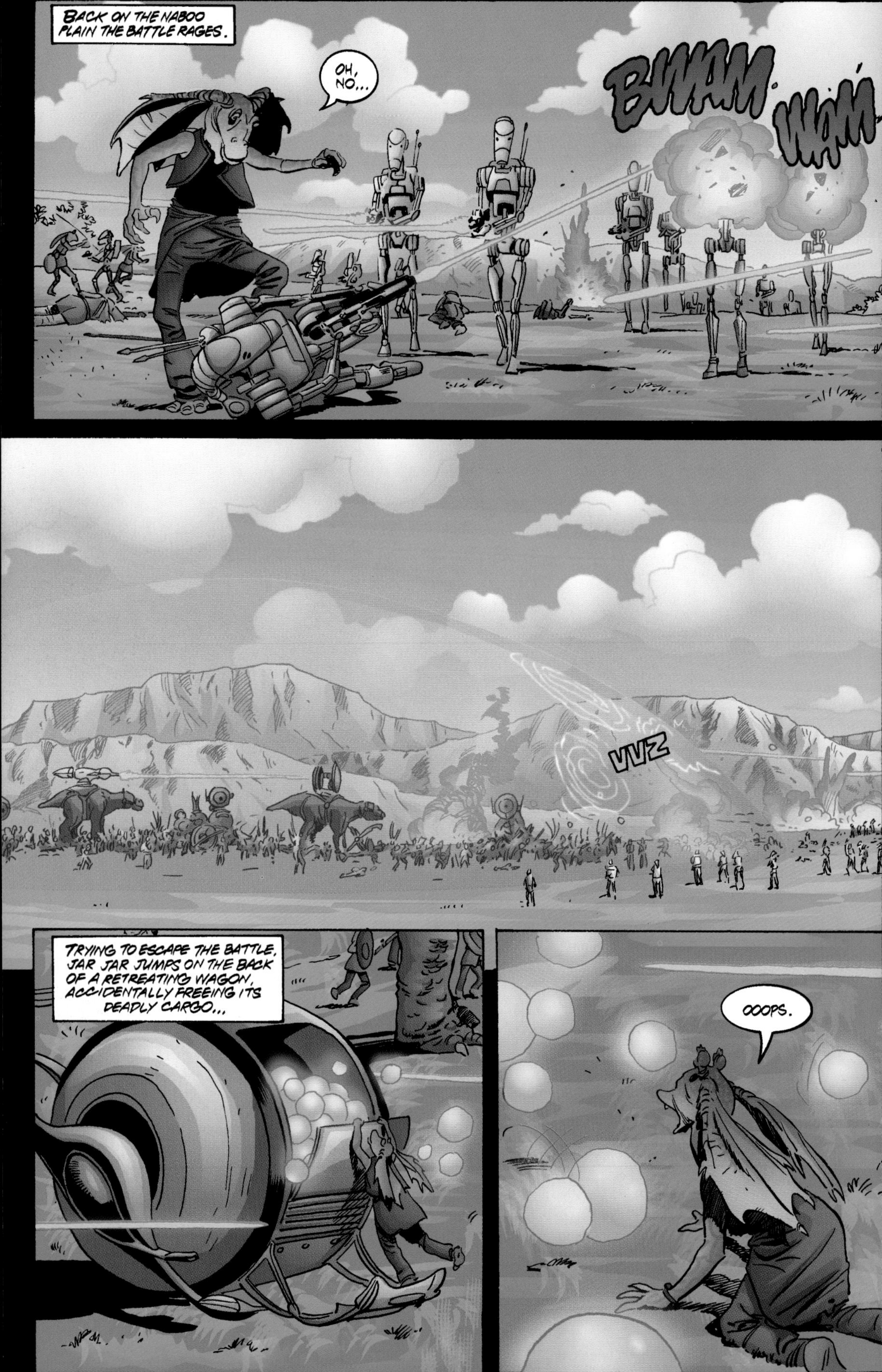

BACK ON THE NABOO PLAIN THE BATTLE RAGES.
OH, NO...
BWAM
WAM
VVZ
TRYING TO ESCAPE THE BATTLE, JAR JAR JUMPS ON THE BACK OF A RETREATING WAGON, ACCIDENTALLY FREEING ITS DEADLY CARGO...
OOOPS.

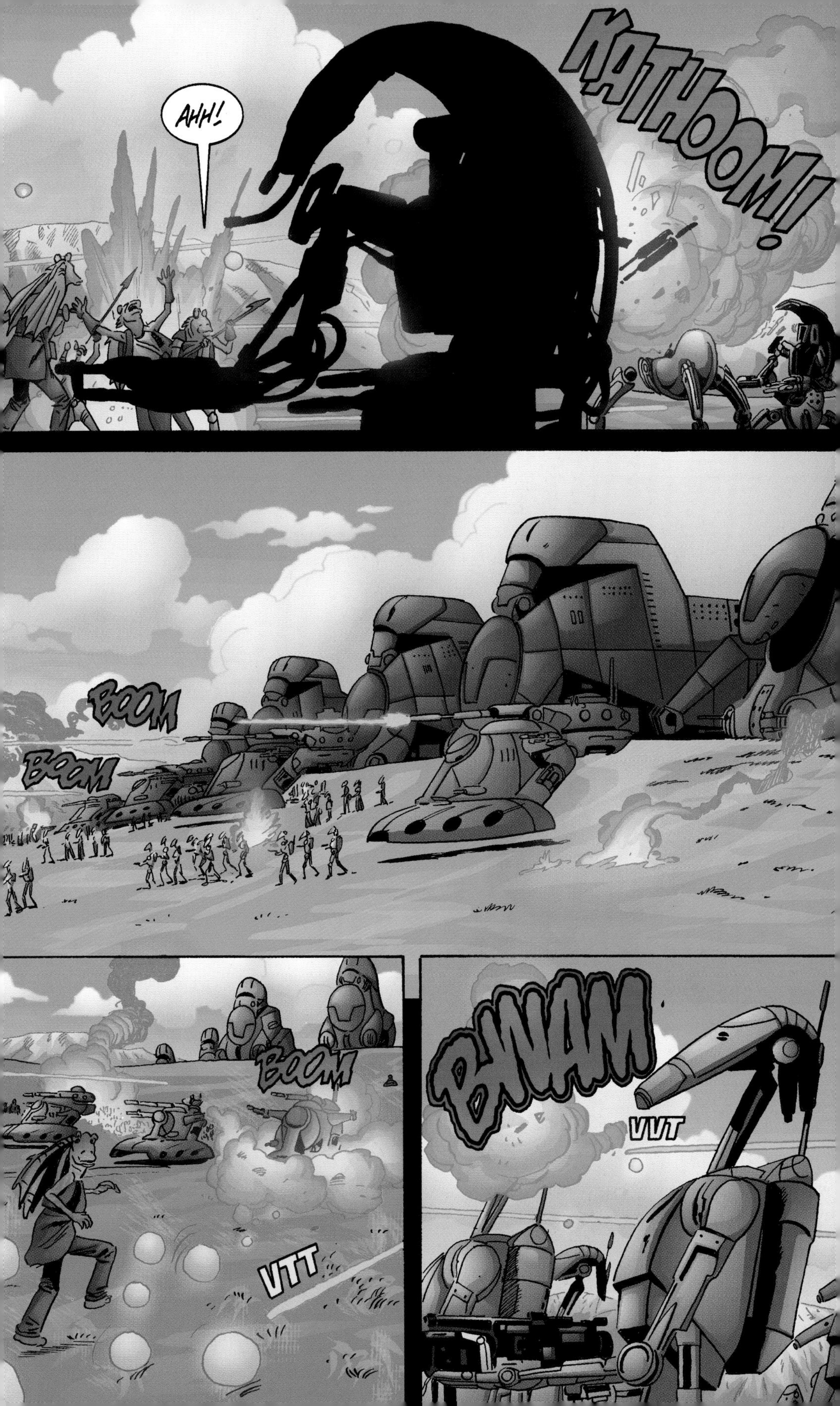
AHH!
KATHOOM!
BOOM
BOOM
BOOM
VTT
BWAM
VVT

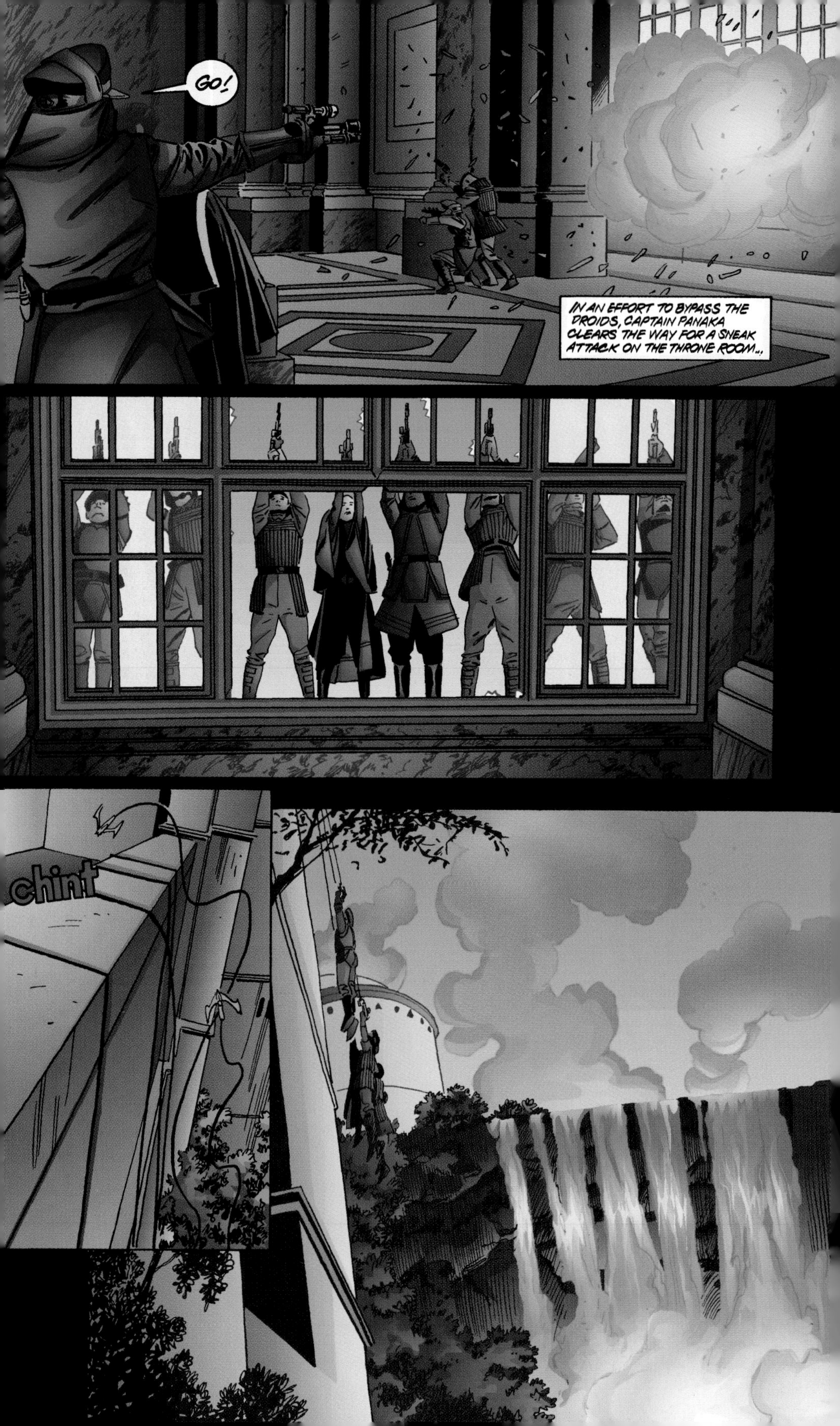
GO!
IN AN EFFORT TO BYPASS THE DROIDS, CAPTAIN PANAKA CLEARS THE WAY FOR A SNEAK ATTACK ON THE THRONE ROOM...
chint

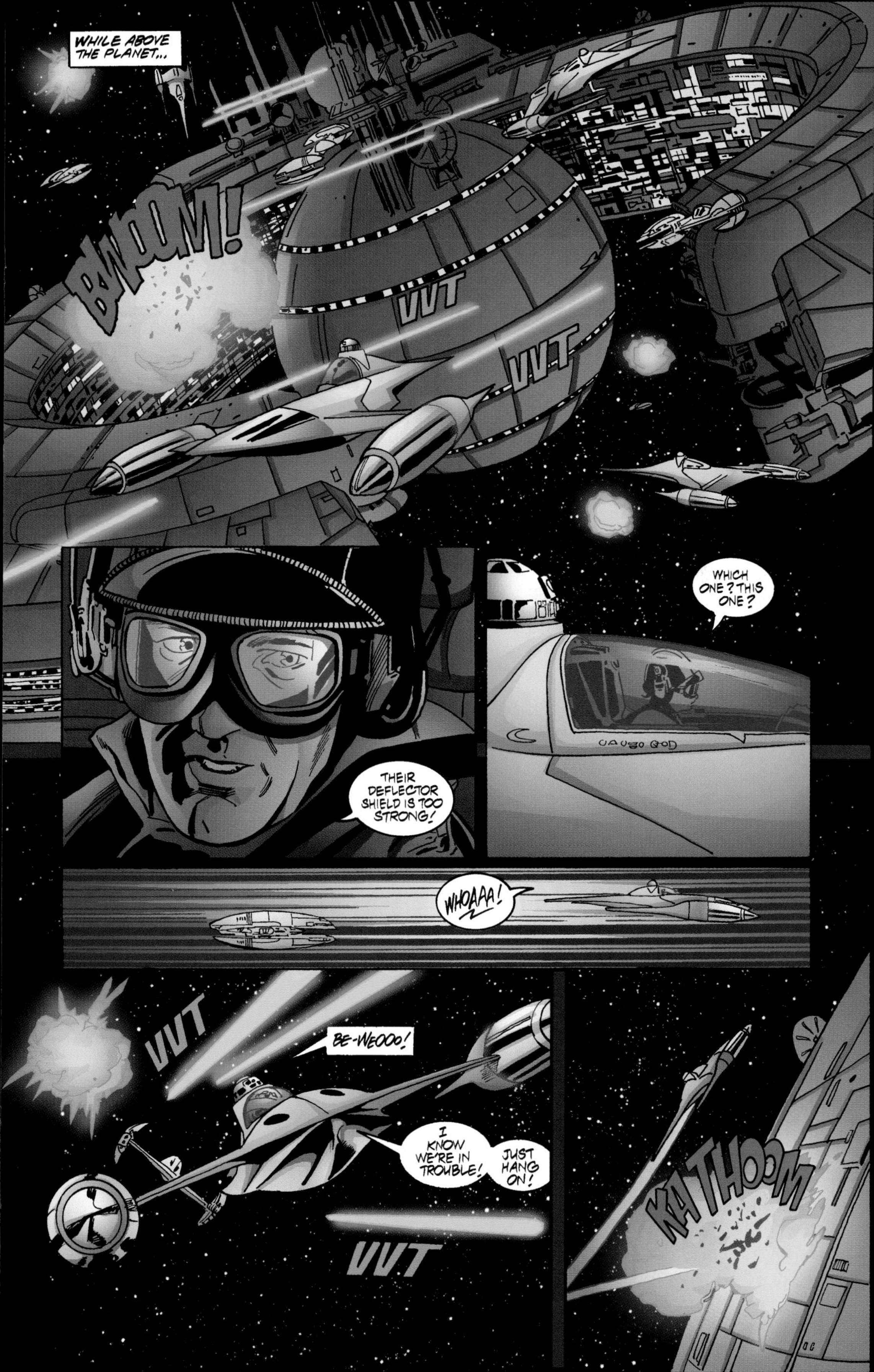
WHILE ABOVE THE PLANET...
BAROOM!
VVT
VVT
THEIR DEFLECTOR SHIELD IS TOO STRONG!
WHICH ONE? THIS ONE?
WHOAAA!
VVT
BE-WEOOO!
I KNOW WE'RE IN TROUBLE!
JUST HANG ON!
VVT
KATHOOM

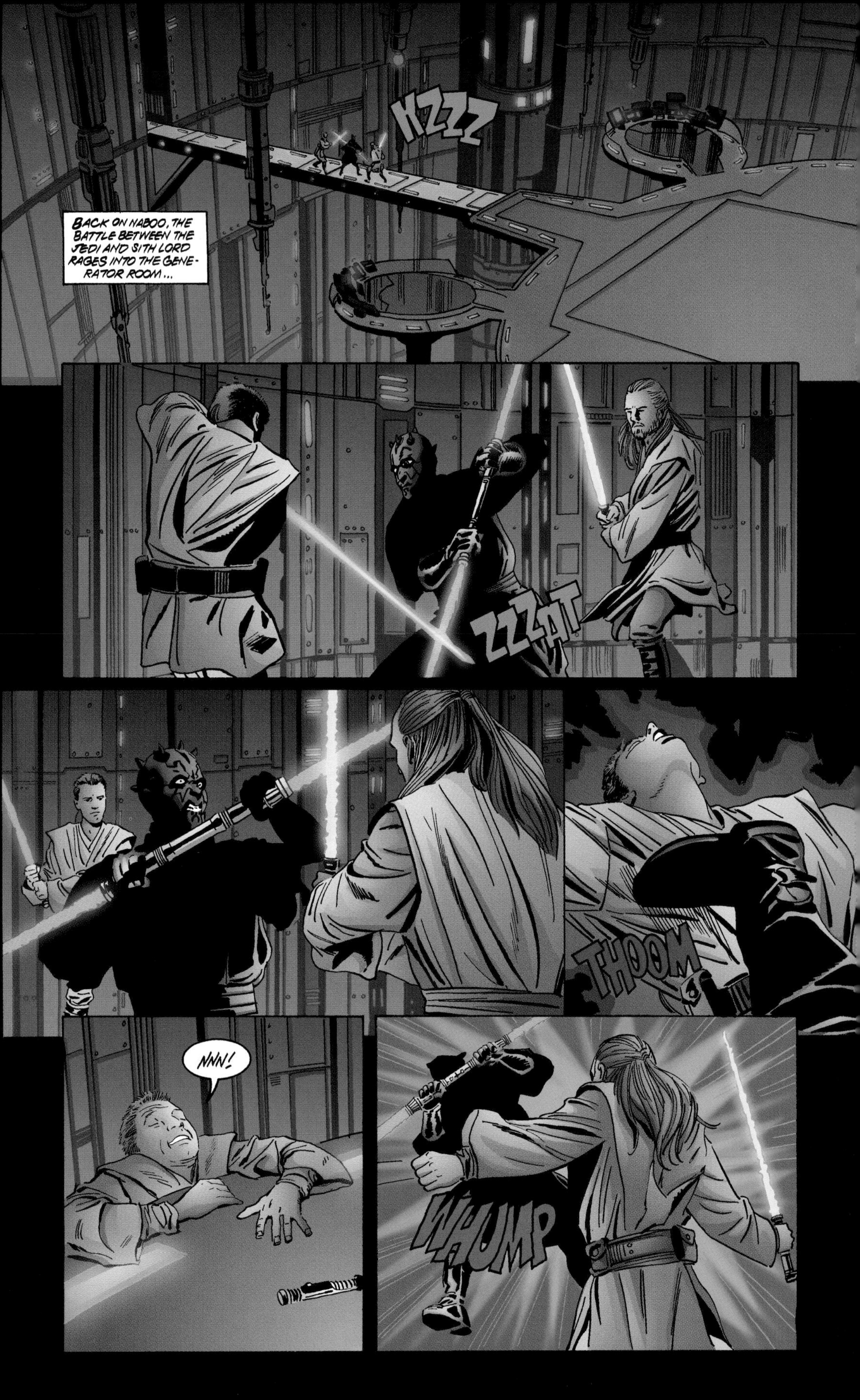
HZZZ
BACK ON NABOO, THE BATTLE BETWEEN THE JEDI AND SITH LORD RAGES INTO THE GENERATOR ROOM...
ZZZAT
THOOM
NNN!
WHUMP

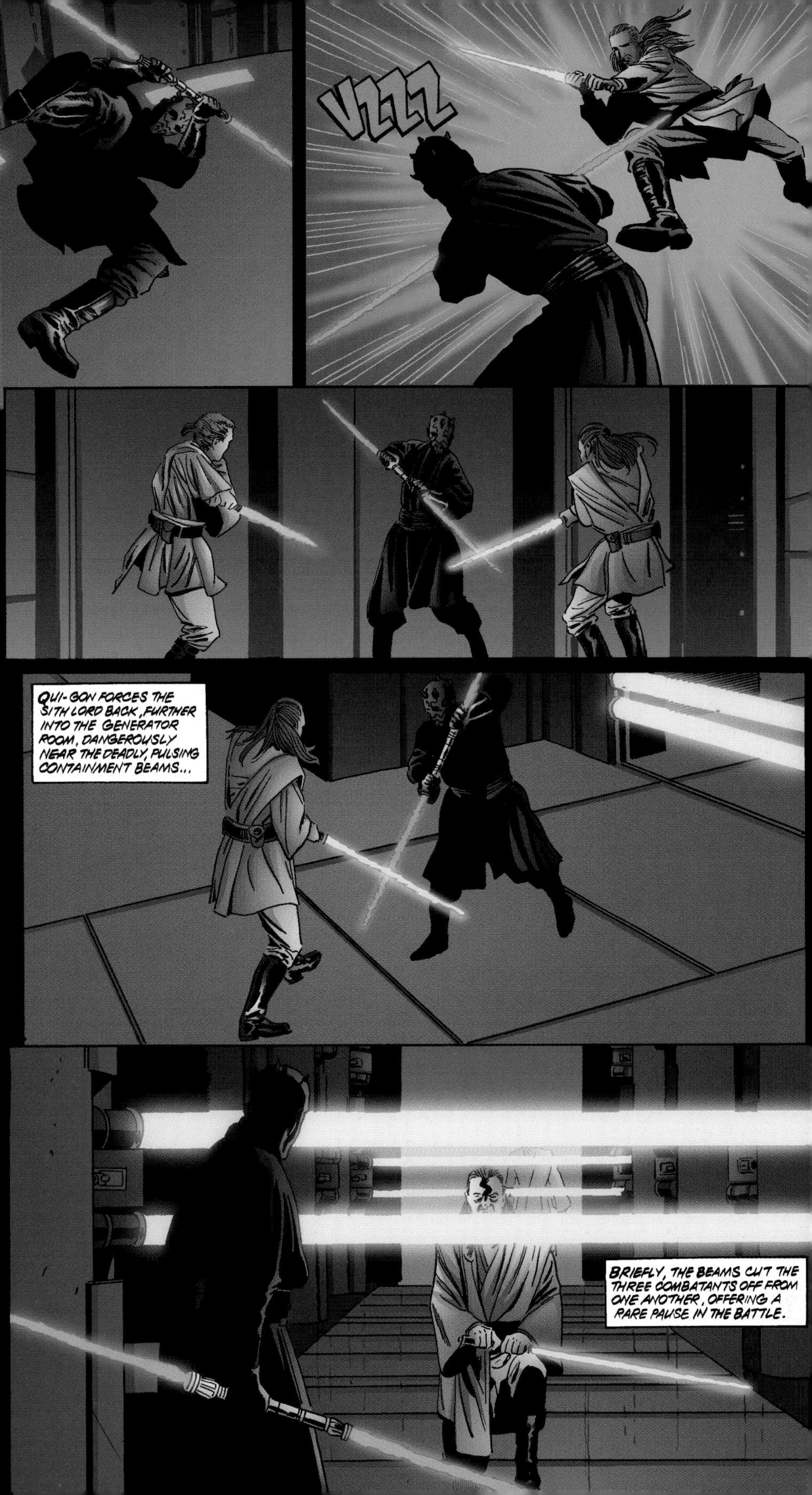
VZZZ
QUI-GON FORCES THE SITH LORD BACK, FURTHER INTO THE GENERATOR ROOM, DANGEROUSLY NEAR THE DEADLY, PULSING CONTAINMENT BEAMS...
BRIEFLY, THE BEAMS CUT THE THREE COMBATANTS OFF FROM ONE ANOTHER, OFFERING A RARE PAUSE IN THE BATTLE.

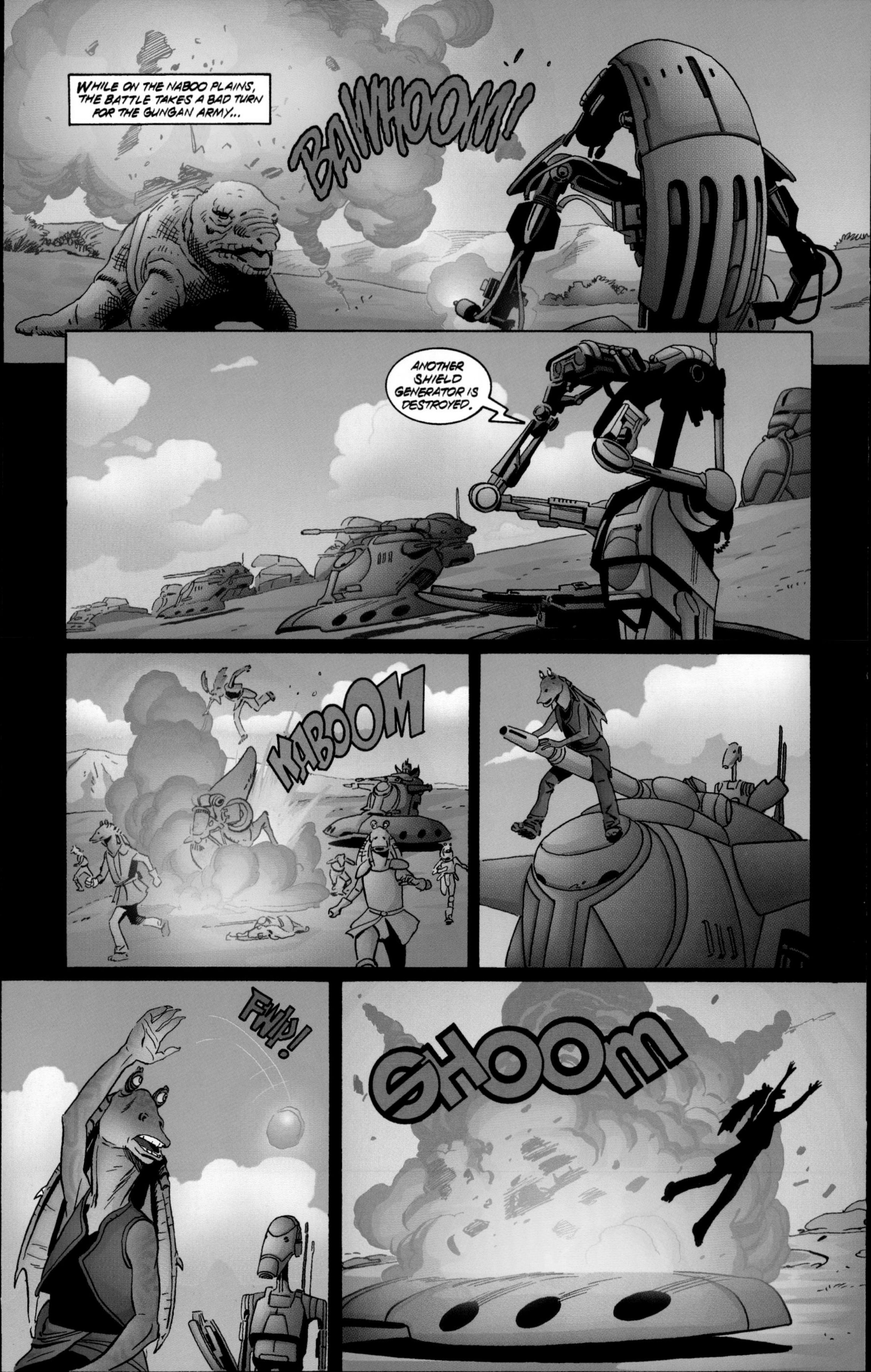
WHILE ON THE NABOO PLAINS, THE BATTLE TAKES A BAD TURN FOR THE GUNGAN ARMY...
BAWHOOM!
ANOTHER SHIELD GENERATOR IS DESTROYED.
KABOOM
FWIP!
SHOOM

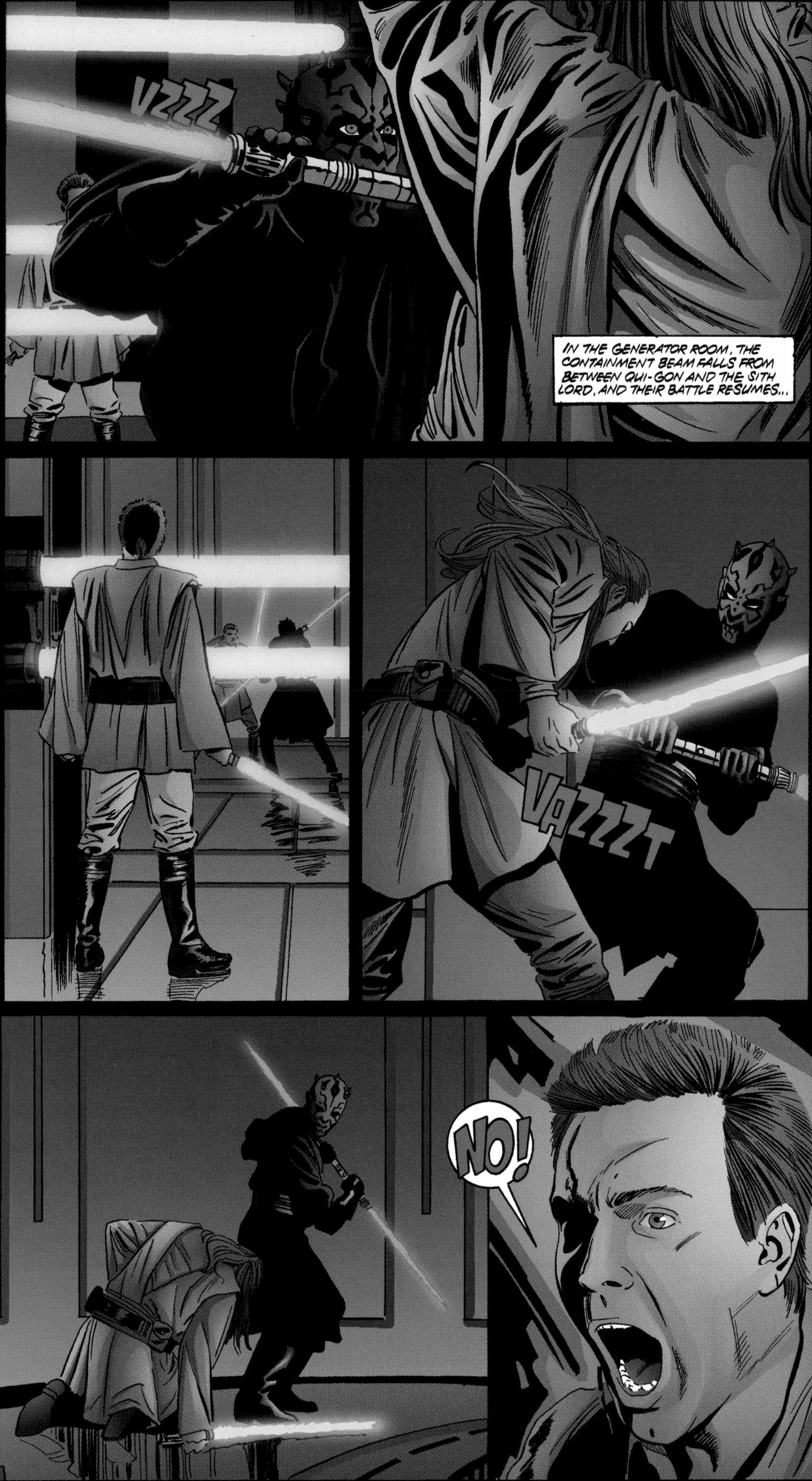
VZZZ
IN THE GENERATOR ROOM, THE CONTAINMENT BEAM FALLS FROM BETWEEN QUI-GON AND THE SITH LORD, AND THEIR BATTLE RESUMES...
VAZZZT
NO!

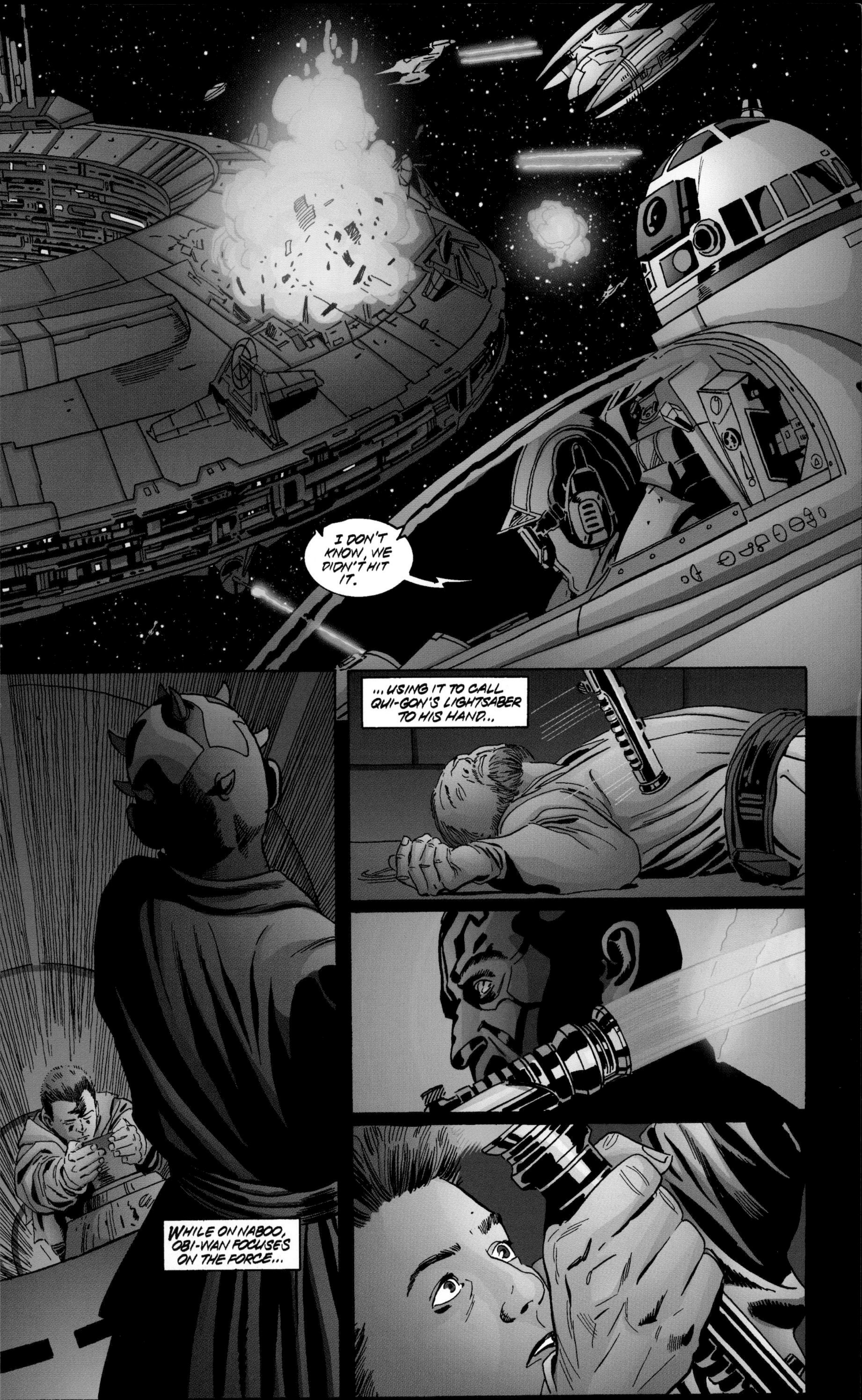
I DON'T KNOW, WE DIDN'T HIT IT.
...USING IT TO CALL QUI-GON'S LIGHTSABER TO HIS HAND...
WHILE ON NABOO, OBI-WAN FOCUSES ON THE FORCE...

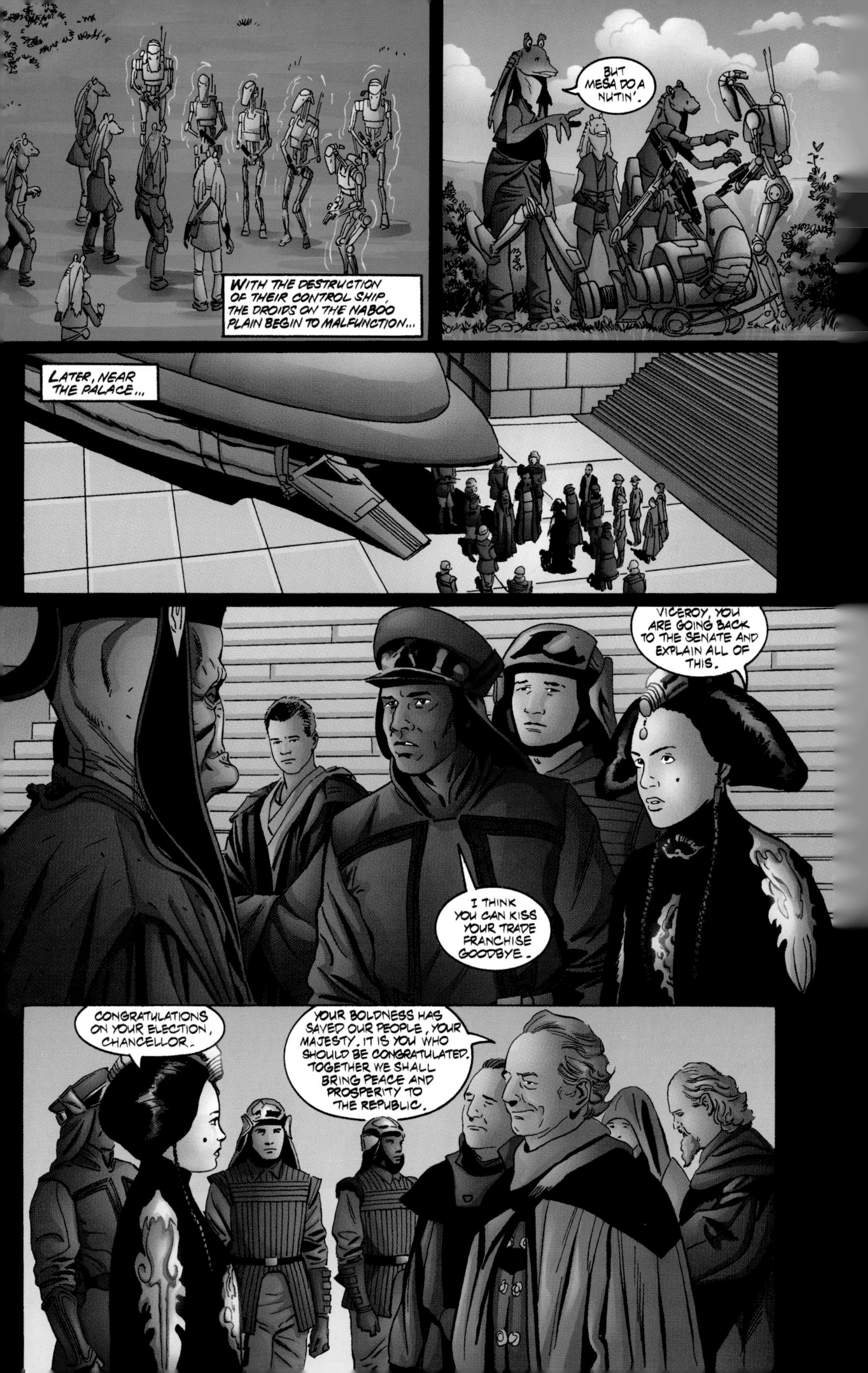
WITH THE DESTRUCTION OF THEIR CONTROL SHIP, THE DROIDS ON THE NABOO PLAIN BEGIN TO MALFUNCTION...
BUT MESA DO A NUTIN'.
LATER, NEAR THE PALACE...
VICEROY, YOU ARE GOING BACK TO THE SENATE AND EXPLAIN ALL OF THIS.
I THINK YOU CAN KISS YOUR TRADE FRANCHISE GOODBYE.
CONGRATULATIONS ON YOUR ELECTION, CHANCELLOR.
YOUR BOLDNESS HAS SAVED OUR PEOPLE, YOUR MAJESTY. IT IS YOU WHO SHOULD BE CONGRATULATED. TOGETHER WE SHALL BRING PEACE AND PROSPERITY TO THE REPUBLIC.

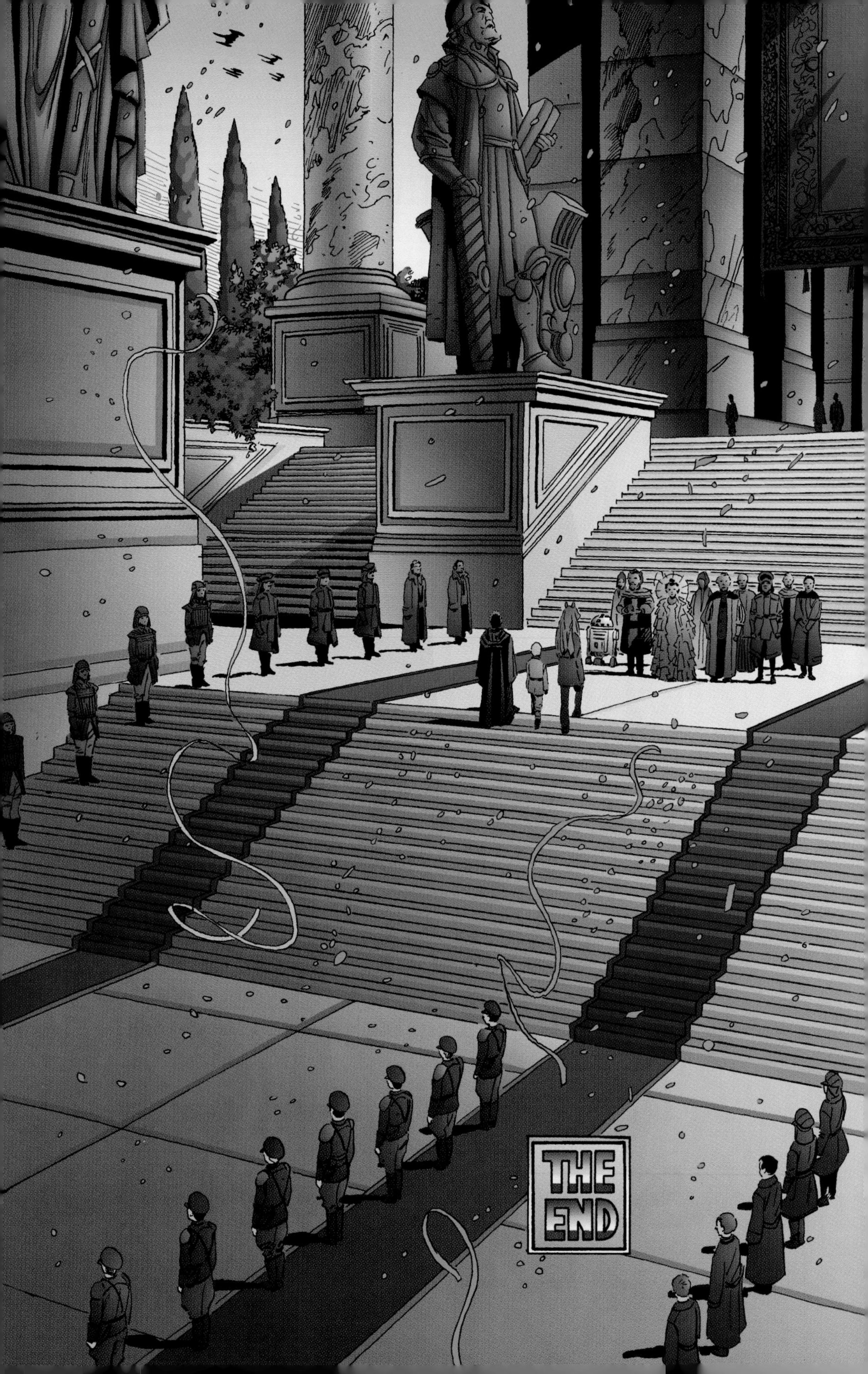
THE END

COVER GALLERY

The following paintings by

HUGH FLEMING

appeared on the front

covers of the serialized

comics editions of

STAR WARS

EPISODE I

THE PHANTOM MENACE™

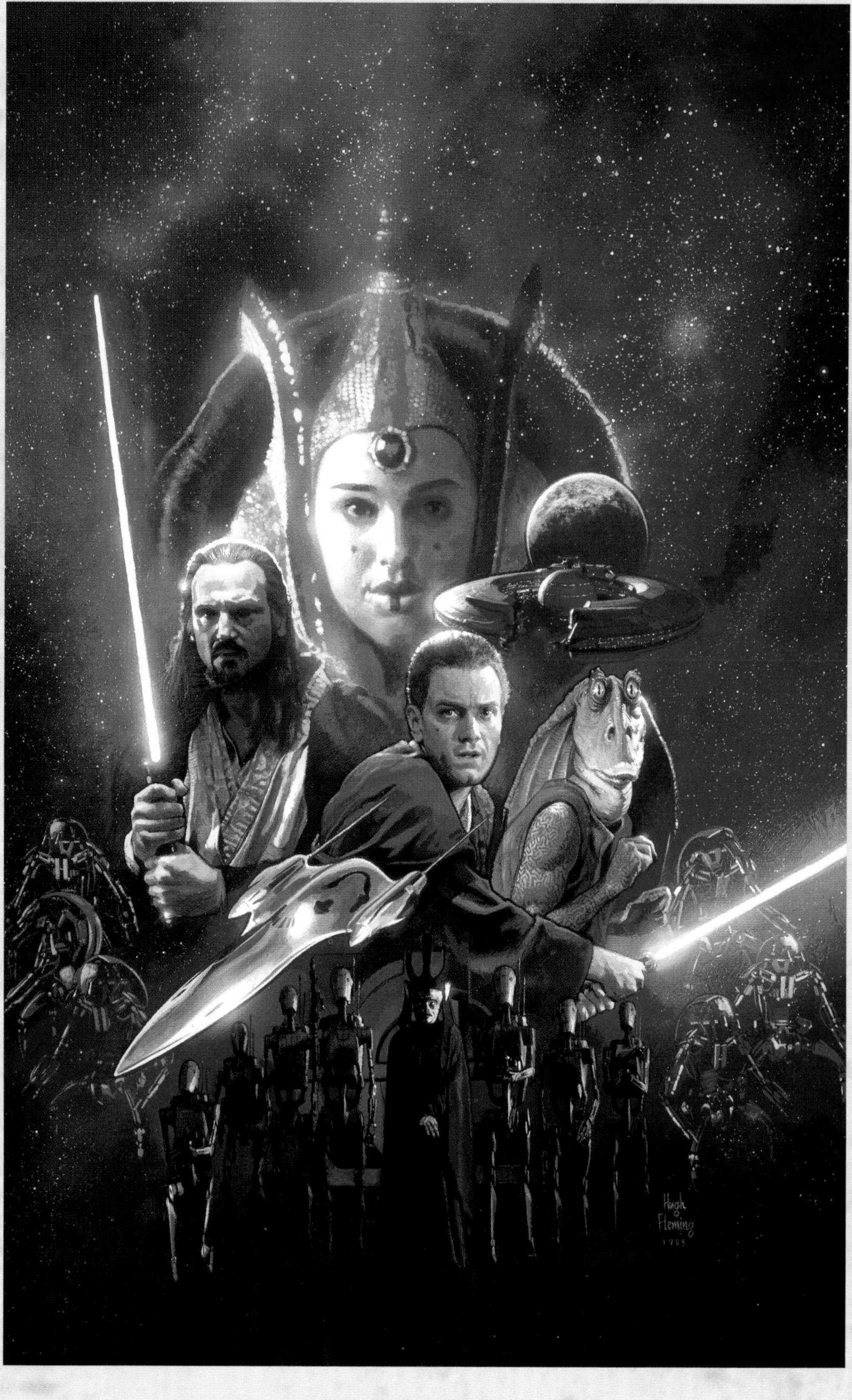

Issue One

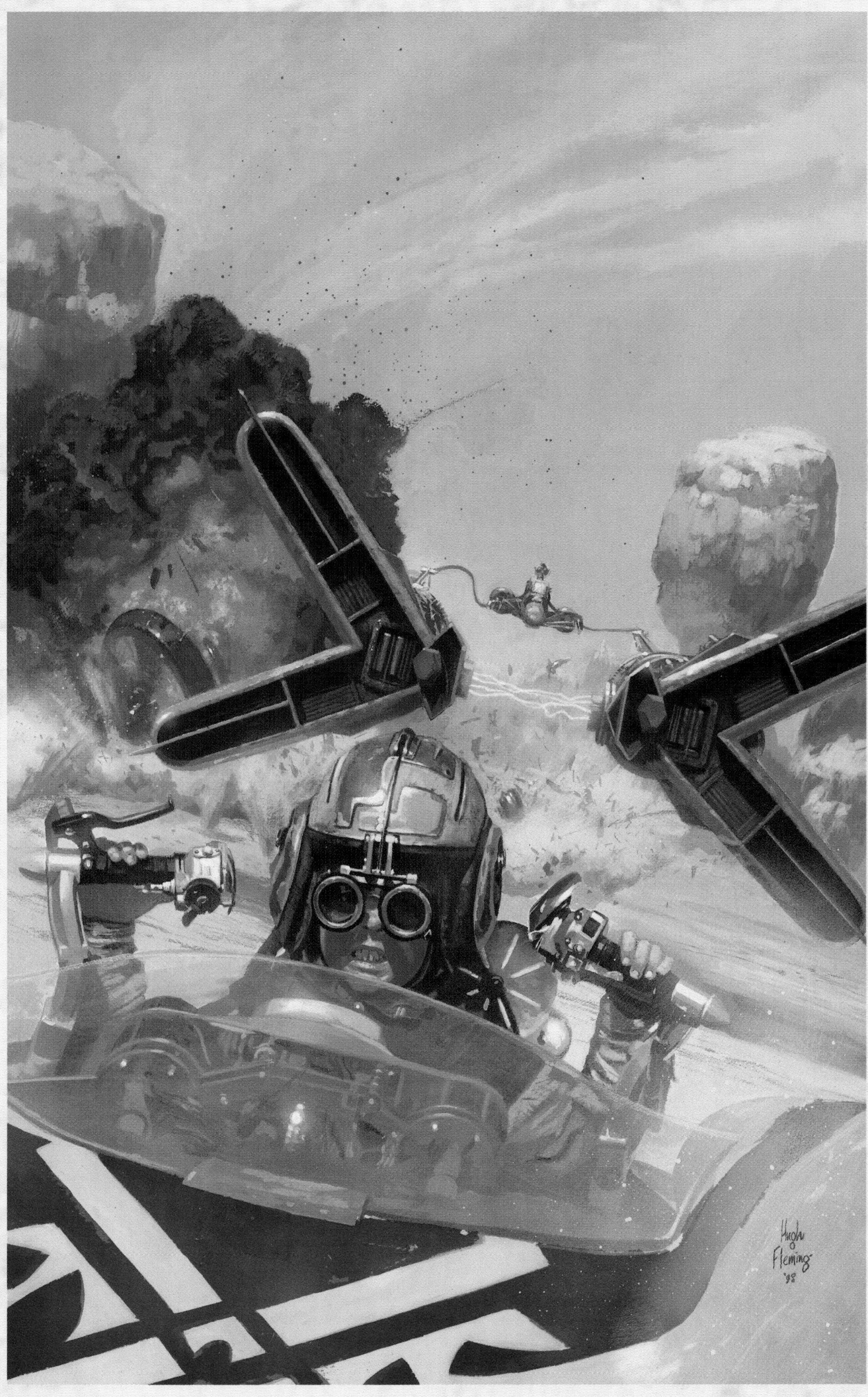
Hugh Fleming '98

Issue Two

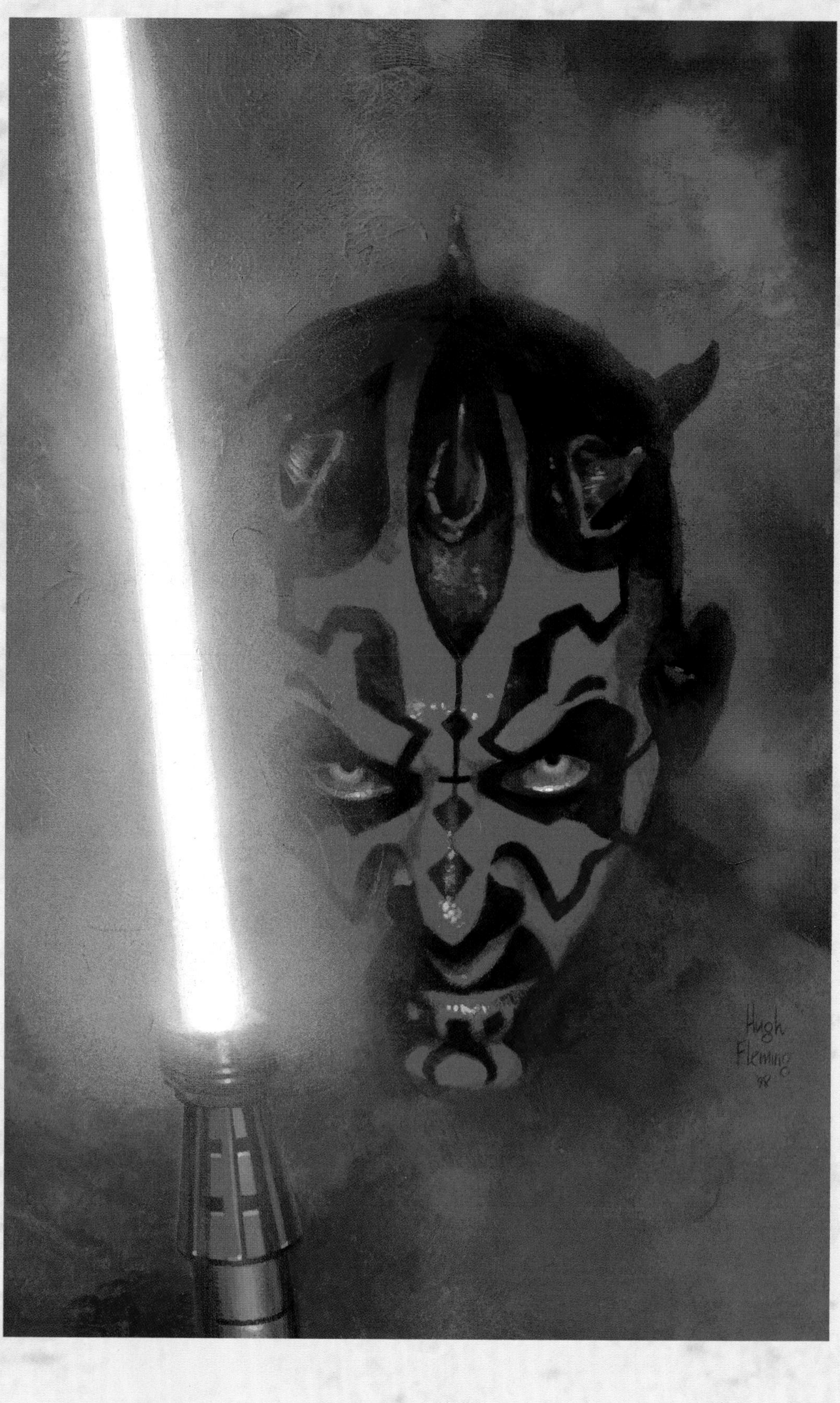
Hugh
Fleming

Issue Three

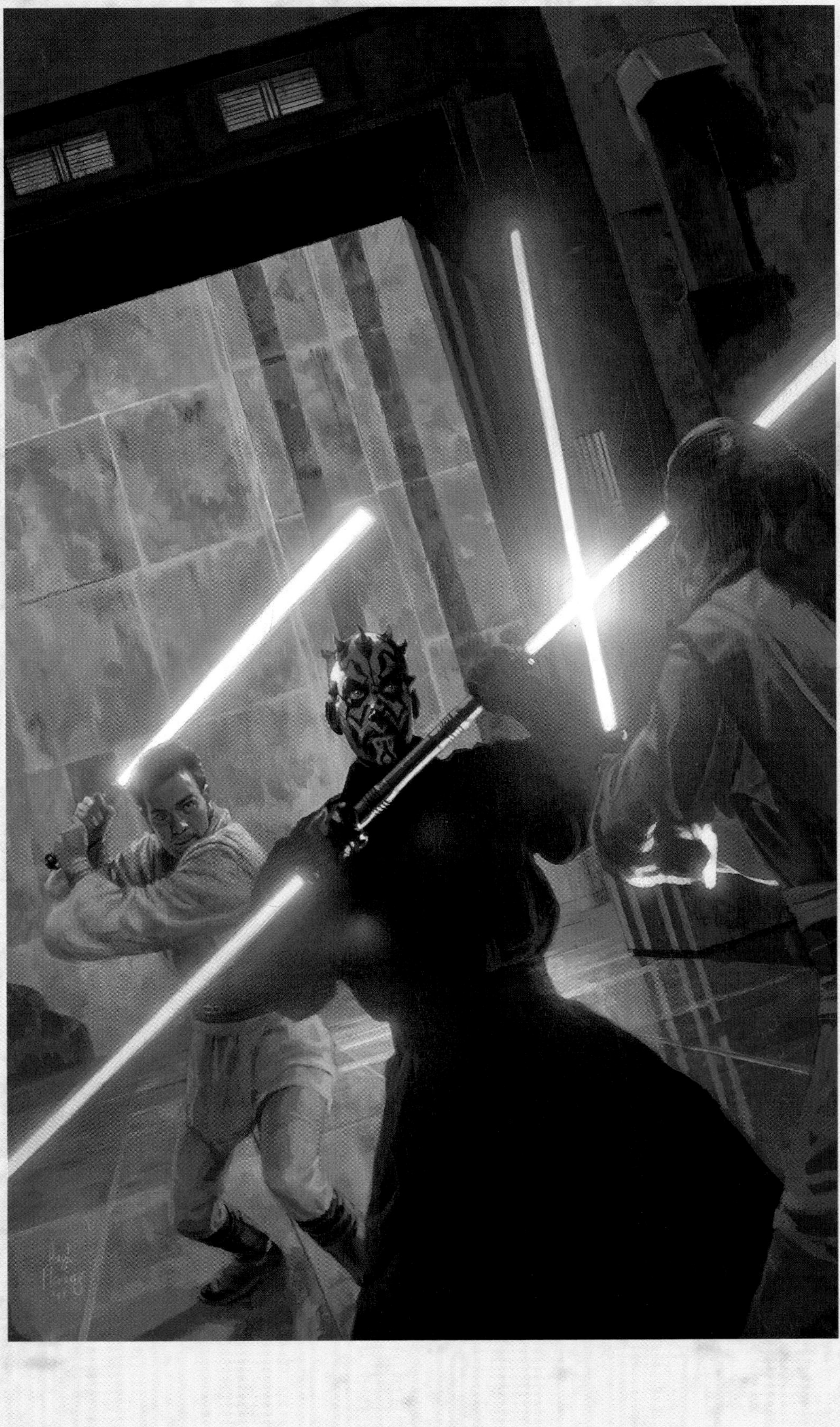

Issue Four

STAR WARS®
EPISODE I
THE PHANTOM MENACE.

Story
GEORGE LUCAS

Script
HENRY GILROY

Penciller
RODOLFO DAMAGGIO

Inker
AL WILLIAMSON

Letterer **STEVE DUTRO**

Colorist **DAVE NESTELLE**

Color Separator **HAROLD MacKINNON**

Cover Artist **RAVENWOOD**

Designer **MARK COX**

Editor **DAVID LAND**

Publisher **MIKE RICHARDSON**

Special thanks to **ALLAN KAUSCH** & **LUCY AUTREY WILSON** at
Lucas Licensing and **TINA MILLS** & **JUSTIN GRAHAM** at Lucasfilm

Advertising sales: (503) 652-8815 x370

Vist the Dark Horse website at **www.darkhorse.com.**

Published by
Dark Horse Comics, Inc.
10956 SE Main Street
Milwaukie, OR 97222

First edition: May 1999
ISBN: 1-56971-359-6

2 4 6 8 10 9 7 5 3 1

PRINTED IN CANADA.

DARK HORSE'S COMPLETE LINE OF STAR WARS SPECIALTY BOOKS

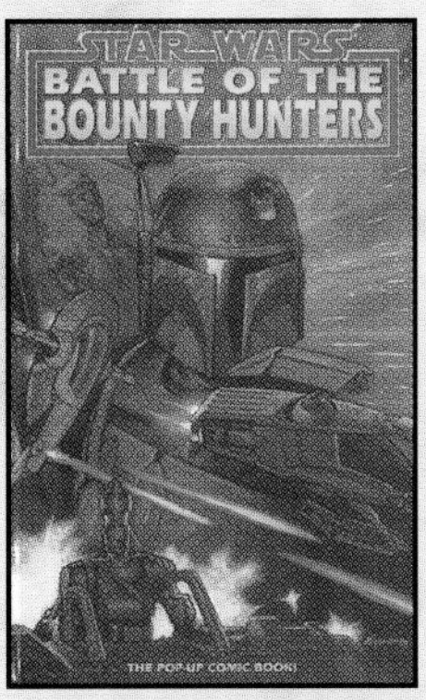
STAR WARS
BATTLE OF THE BOUNTY HUNTERS
THE POP-UP COMIC BOOKS

BATTLE OF THE BOUNTY HUNTERS
POP-UP COMIC BOOK
ISBN: 1-56971-129-1 $17.95

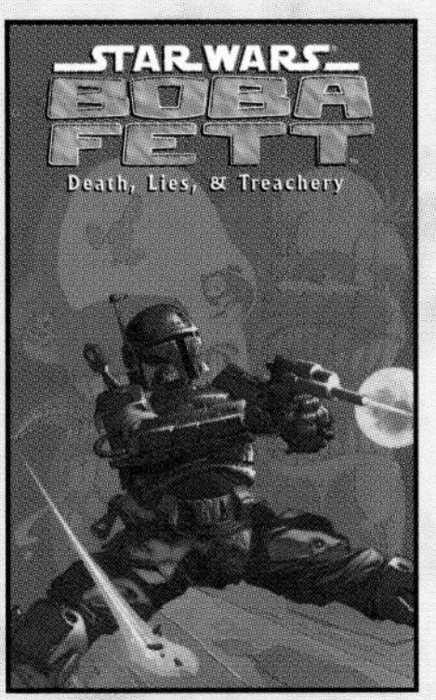
STAR WARS
BOBA FETT
Death, Lies, & Treachery

BOBA FETT
DEATH , LIES, & TREACHERY
ISBN: 1-56971-311-1 $12.95

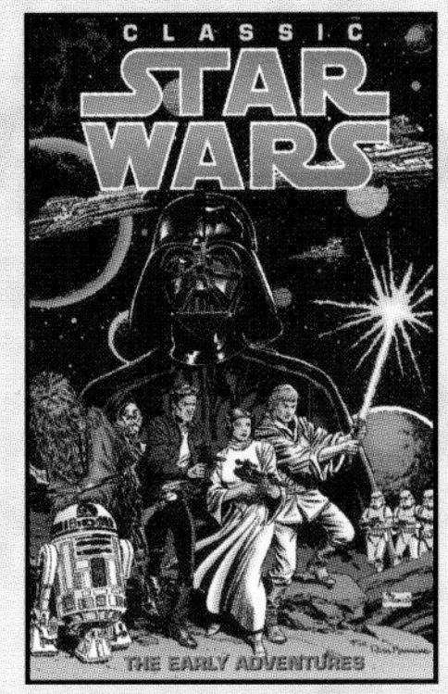
CLASSIC
STAR WARS
THE EARLY ADVENTURES

CLASSIC STAR WARS
THE EARLY ADVENTURES
ISBN: 1-56971-178-X $19.95

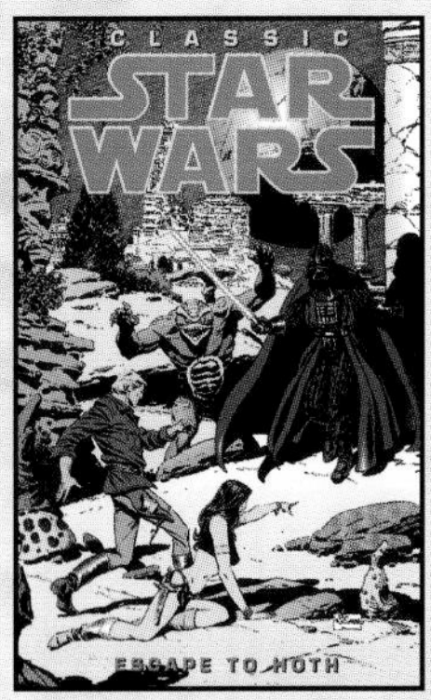
CLASSIC
STAR WARS
ESCAPE TO HOTH

CLASSIC STAR WARS
ESCAPE TO HOTH
ISBN: 1-56971-093-7 $16.95

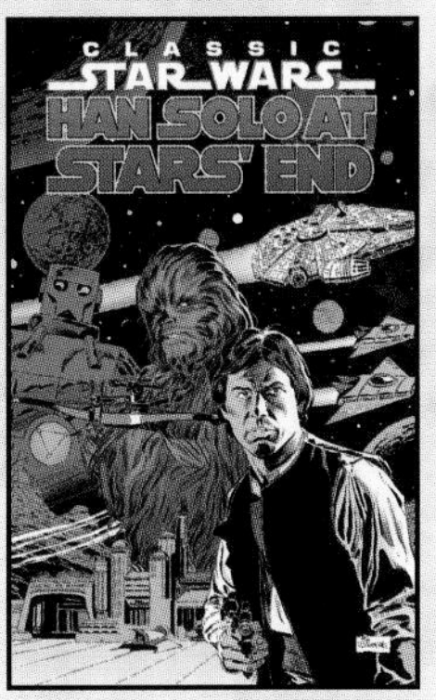
CLASSIC
STAR WARS
HAN SOLO AT STARS' END

CLASSIC STAR WARS
HAN SOLO AT STARS' END
ISBN: 1-56971-254-9 $6.95

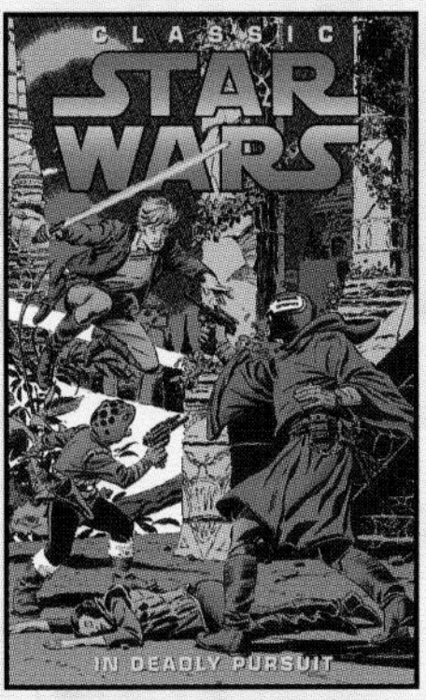
CLASSIC
STAR WARS
IN DEADLY PURSUIT

CLASSIC STAR WARS
IN DEADLY PURSUIT
ISBN: 1-56971-109-7 $16.95

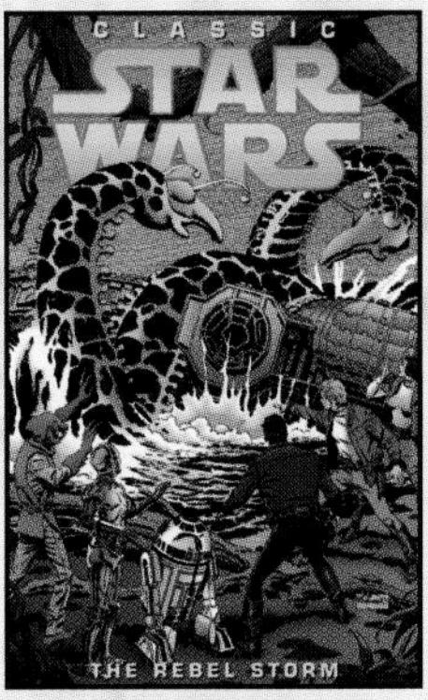
CLASSIC
STAR WARS
THE REBEL STORM

CLASSIC STAR WARS
THE REBEL STORM
ISBN: 1-56971-106-2 $16.95

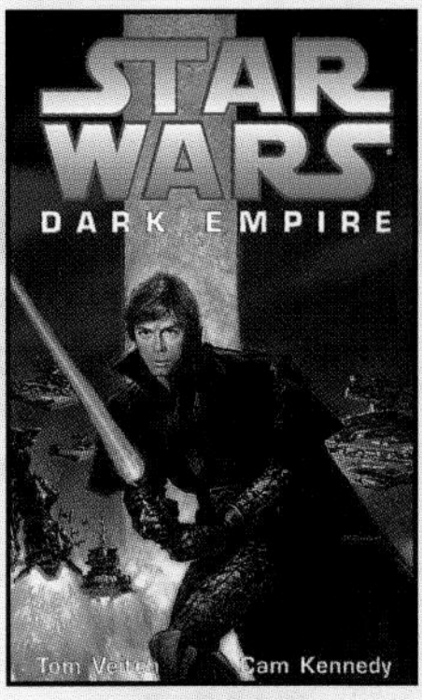
STAR WARS
DARK EMPIRE
Cam Kennedy

DARK EMPIRE
ISBN: 1-56971-073-2 $17.95

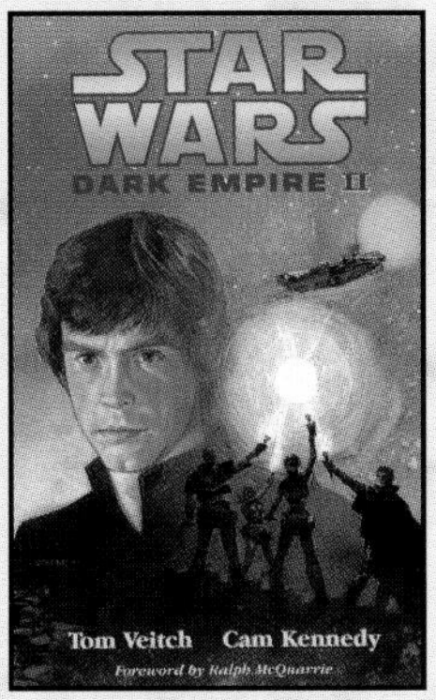
STAR WARS
DARK EMPIRE II
Tom Veitch Cam Kennedy
Foreword by Ralph McQuarrie

DARK EMPIRE II
ISBN: 1-56971-119-4 $17.95

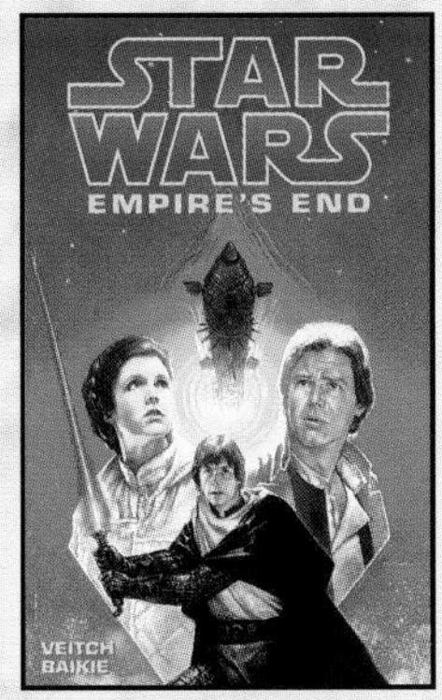
STAR WARS
EMPIRE'S END
VEITCH
BAIKIE

EMPIRE'S END
ISBN: 1-56971-306-5 $5.95

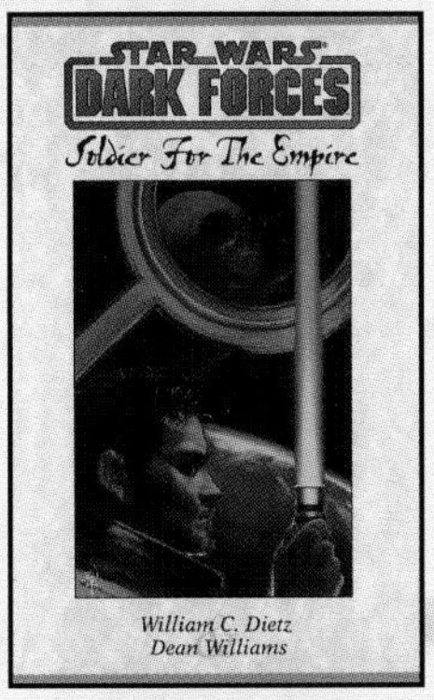
STAR WARS
DARK FORCES
Soldier For The Empire
William C. Dietz
Dean Williams

DARK FORCES
SOLDIER FOR THE EMPIRE
ISBN: 1-56971-155-0 $24.95

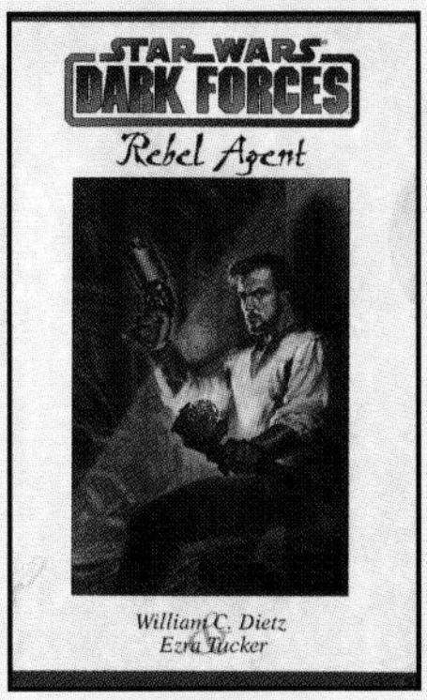
STAR WARS
DARK FORCES
Rebel Agent
William C. Dietz
Ezra Tucker

DARK FORCES
REBEL AGENT
ISBN: 1-56971-156-9 $24.95

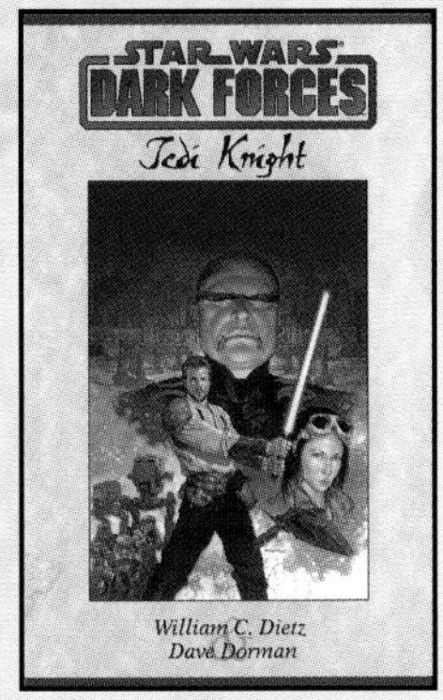
STAR WARS
DARK FORCES
Jedi Knight
William C. Dietz
Dave Dorman

DARK FORCES
JEDI KNIGHT
ISBN: 1-56971-157-7 $24.95

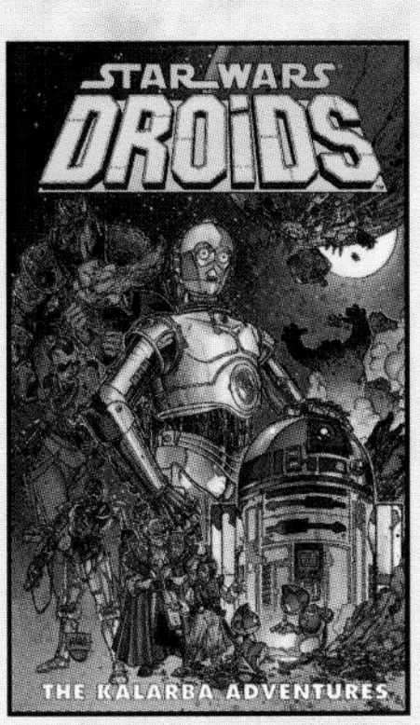
STAR WARS
DROIDS
THE KALARBA ADVENTURES

DROIDS
THE KALARBA ADVENTURES
ISBN: 1-56971-064-3 $17.95

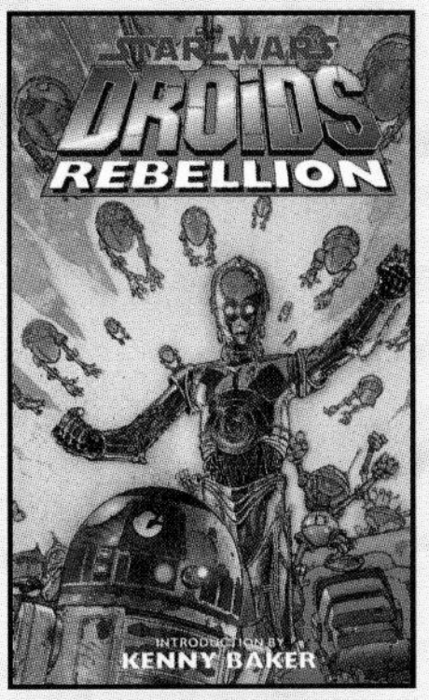
STAR WARS
DROIDS
REBELLION
INTRODUCTION BY
KENNY BAKER

DROIDS
REBELLION
ISBN: 1-56971-224-7 $14.95

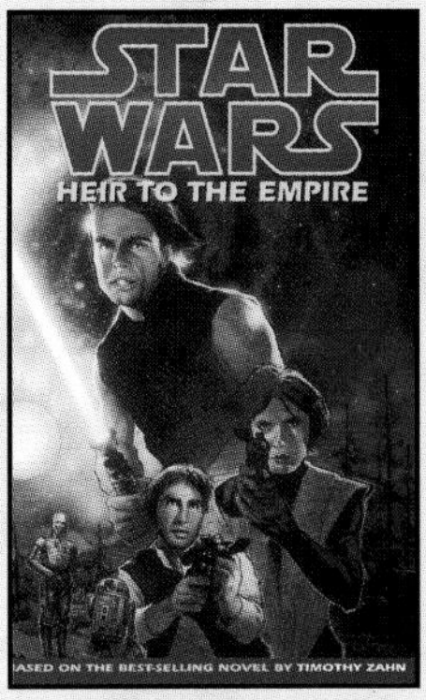
STAR WARS
HEIR TO THE EMPIRE

HEIR TO THE EMPIRE
ISBN: 1-56971-202-6 $19.95

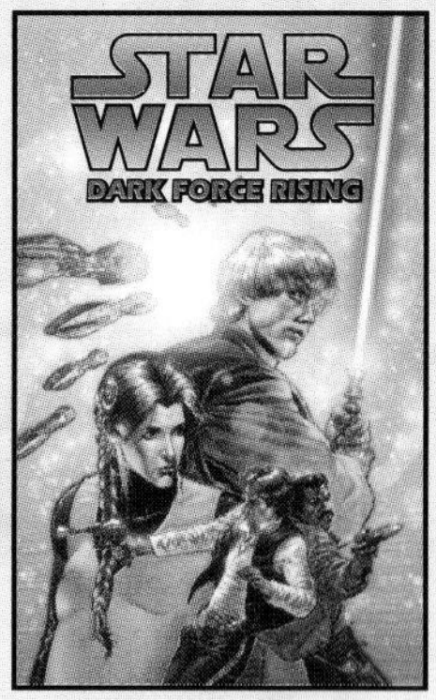
STAR WARS
DARK FORCE RISING

DARK FORCE RISING
ISBN: 1-56971-269-7 $17.95

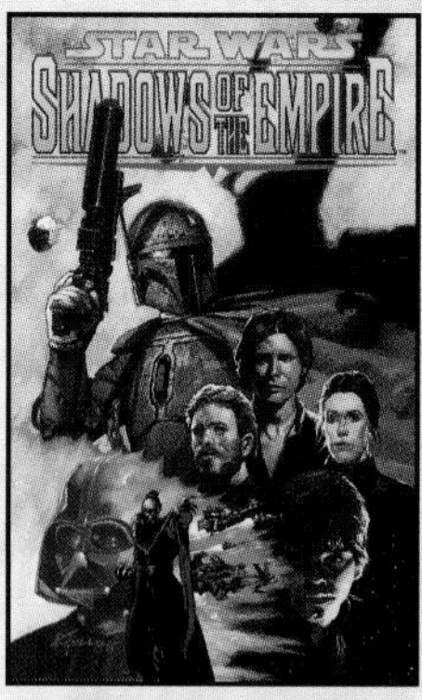
STAR WARS
SHADOWS OF THE EMPIRE

SHADOWS OF THE EMPIRE
ISBN: 1-56971-183-6 $17.95

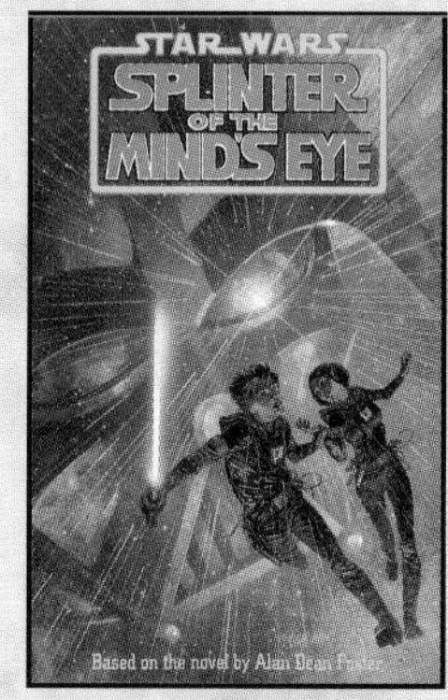
STAR WARS
SPLINTER OF THE MIND'S EYE
Based on the novel by Alan Dean Foster

SPLINTER OF THE MIND'S EYE
ISBN: 1-56971-223-9 $14.95

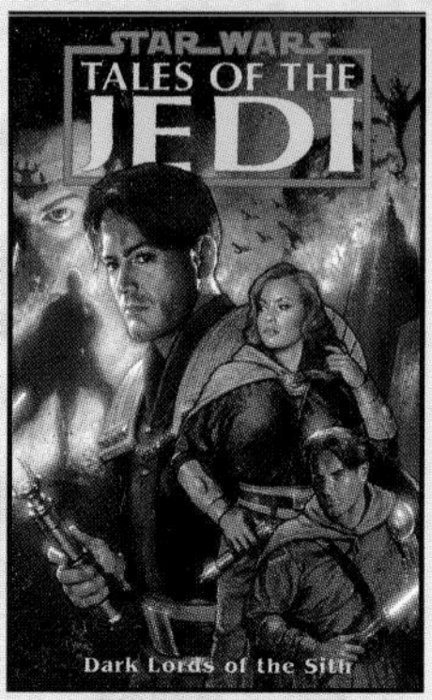
STAR WARS
TALES OF THE JEDI
Dark Lords of the Sith

TALES OF THE JEDI
DARK LORDS OF THE SITH
ISBN: 1-56971-095-3 $17.95

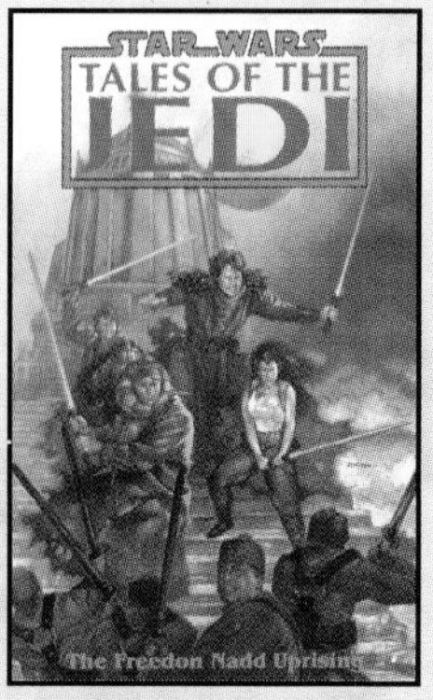
STAR WARS
TALES OF THE JEDI

TALES OF THE JEDI
THE FREEDON NADD UPRISING
ISBN: 1-56971-307-3 $5.95

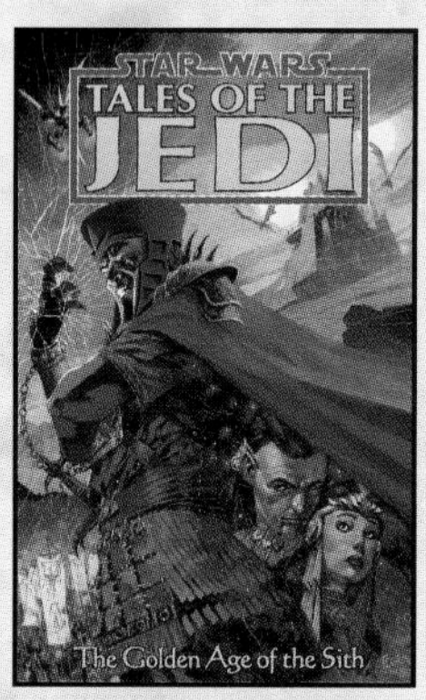
STAR WARS
TALES OF THE JEDI
The Golden Age of the Sith

TALES OF THE JEDI
THE GOLDEN AGE OF THE SITH
ISBN: 1-56971-229-8 $16.95

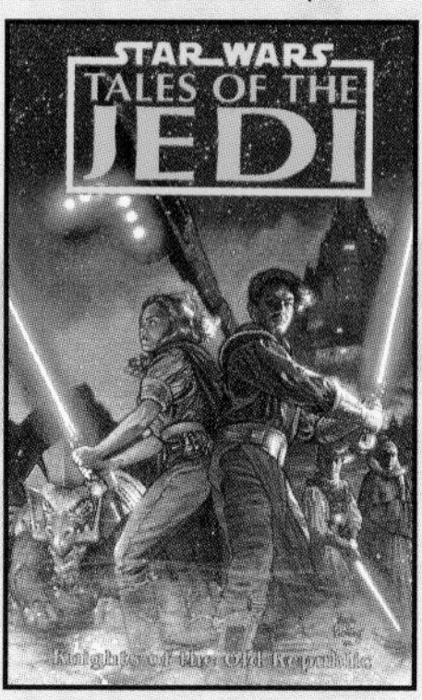
STAR WARS
TALES OF THE JEDI

TALES OF THE JEDI
KNIGHTS OF THE OLD REPUBLIC
ISBN: 1-56971-020-1 $14.95

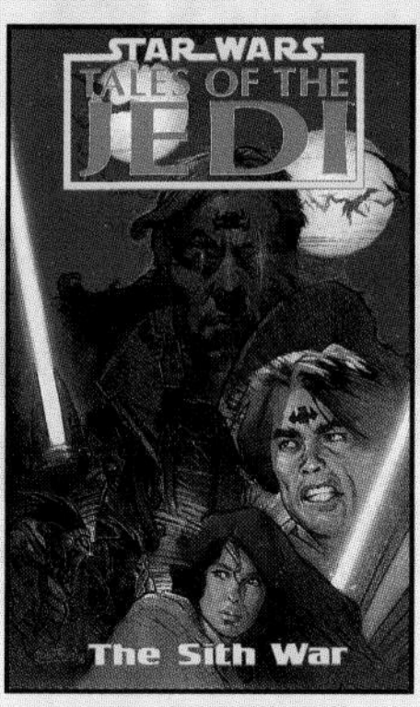
STAR WARS
TALES OF THE JEDI
The Sith War

TALES OF THE JEDI
THE SITH WAR
ISBN: 1-56971-173-9 $17.95

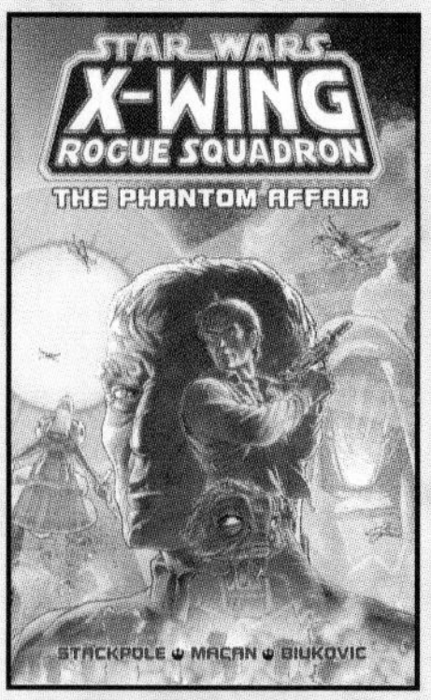
STAR WARS
X-WING
ROGUE SQUADRON
THE PHANTOM AFFAIR
STACKPOLE MACAN BIUKOVIC

X-WING ROGUE SQUADRON
THE PHANTOM AFFAIR
ISBN: 1-56971-251-4 $12.95

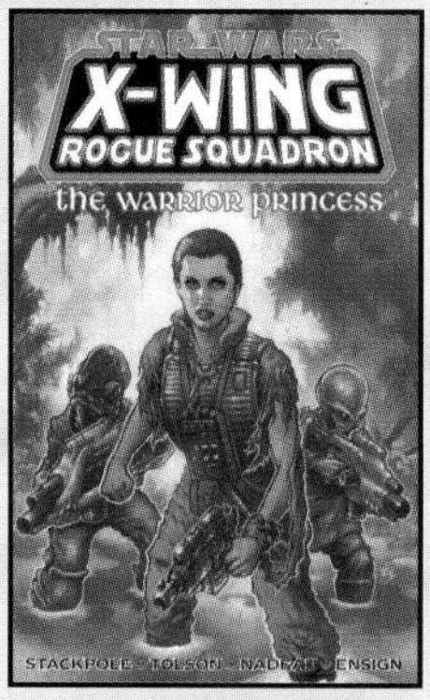
STAR WARS
X-WING
ROGUE SQUADRON
the warrior princess

X-WING ROGUE SQUADRON
THE WARRIOR PRINCESS
ISBN: 1-56971-330-8 $12.95

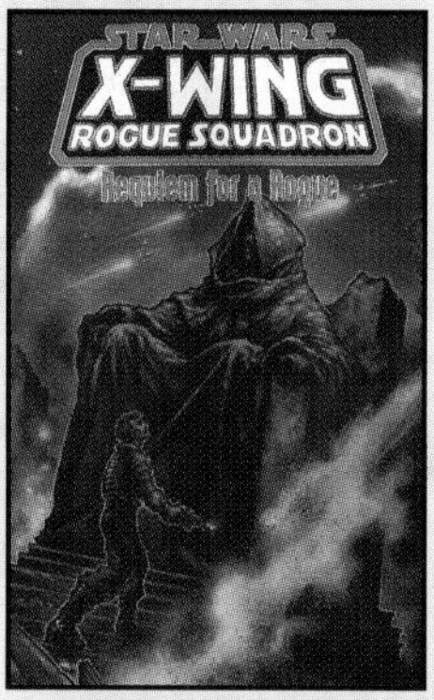
STAR WARS
X-WING
ROGUE SQUADRON
Requiem for a Rogue

X-WING ROGUE SQUADRON
REQUIEM FOR A ROGUE
ISBN: 1-56971-331-6 $12.95

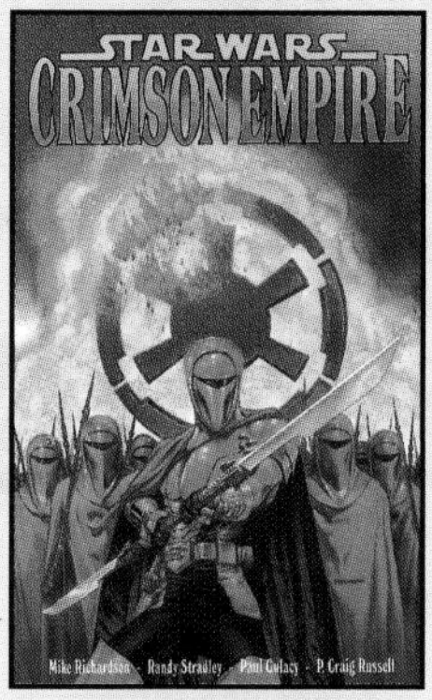
STAR WARS
CRIMSON EMPIRE

CRIMSON EMPIRE
ISBN: 1-56971-355-3 $17.95

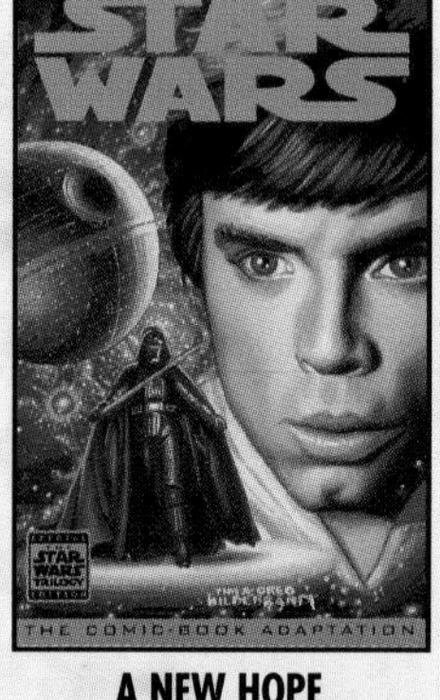
STAR WARS
THE COMIC-BOOK ADAPTATION

A NEW HOPE
THE SPECIAL EDITION
ISBN: 1-56971-213-1 $9.95

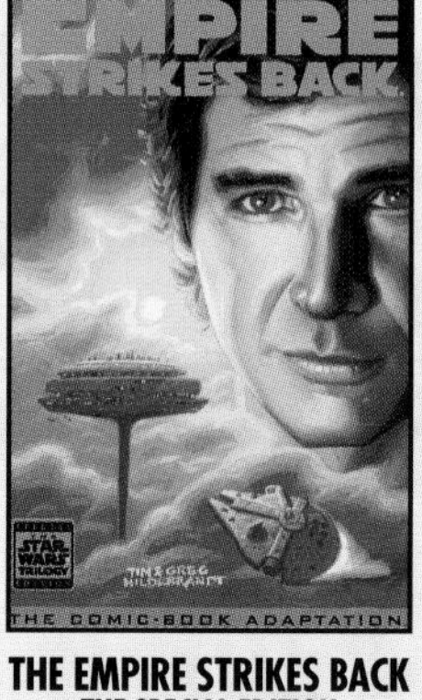
THE EMPIRE STRIKES BACK
THE COMIC-BOOK ADAPTATION

THE EMPIRE STRIKES BACK
THE SPECIAL EDITION
ISBN: 1-56971-234-4 $9.95

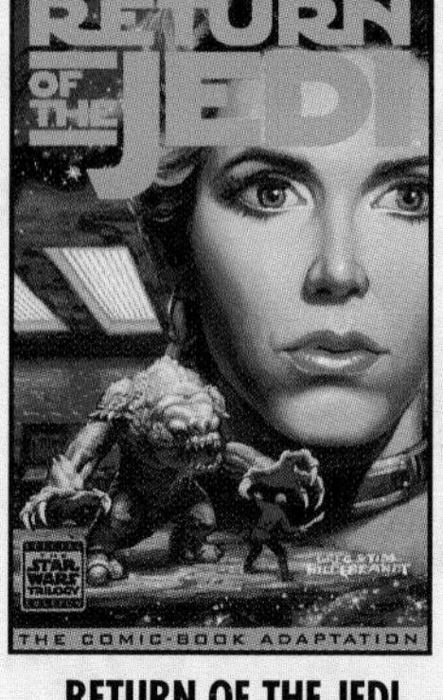
RETURN OF THE JEDI
THE COMIC-BOOK ADAPTATION

RETURN OF THE JEDI
THE SPECIAL EDITION
ISBN: 1-56971-235-2 $9.95

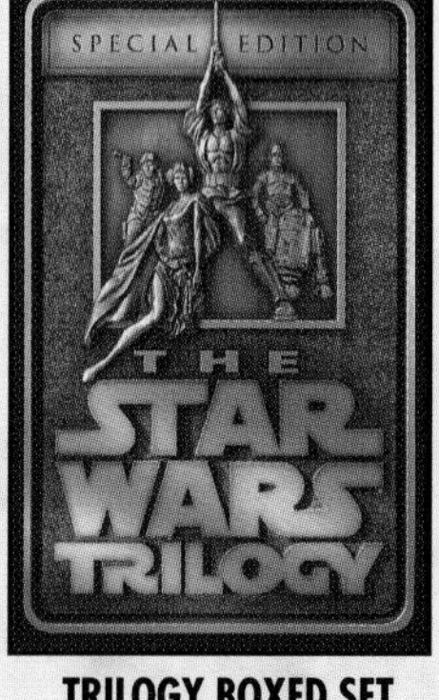
SPECIAL EDITION
THE STAR WARS TRILOGY

TRILOGY BOXED SET
THE SPECIAL EDITION
ISBN: 1-56971-257-3 $29.85

AVAILABLE AT YOUR LOCAL COMICS SHOP OR BOOKSTORE.
Or to order direct: •on the web: www.darkhorse.com •e-mail: mailorder@darkhorse.com
•phone: 1-800-862-0052 or (503) 652-9701 Mon.-Sat. 9 A.M. to 5 P.M. Pacific Time